THE EVOLUTION CONSPIRACY

Caryl Matrisciana & Roger Oakland

D0012163

HARVEST HOUSE PUBLISHERS
Eugene, Oregon 97402

Except where otherwise indicated, all Scripture quotations are taken from the King James Version of the Bible.

Verses marked NASB are taken from the New American Standard Bible, Copyright © The Lockman Foundation 1960, 1962, 1963, 1968, 1971, 1972, 1973, 1975, 1977. Used by permission.

THE EVOLUTION CONSPIRACY

Copyright © 1991 by Harvest House Publishers
Eugene, Oregon 97402

Library of Congress Cataloging-in-Publication Data

Matrisciana, Caryl, 1947–
    The evolution conspiracy / Caryl Matrisciana, Roger Oakland.
    ISBN 0-89081-939-4
    1. Evolution (Biology)—Religious aspects—Christianity—Controversial literature.   2. Creationism.   3. Secularism—United States—Controversial literature.   4. United States—Moral conditions.   5. Church and state—United States.   6. New Age movement—Controversial literature.   I. Oakland, Roger, 1947– .
II. Title.
BT712.M38   1991   91-16407
231.7′65—dc20   CIP

All rights reserved. No portion of this book may be reproduced in any form without the written permission of the Publisher.

Printed in the United States of America.

Worthy art Thou, our Lord and our God, to receive glory and honor and power; for Thou didst create all things, and because of Thy will they existed, and were created.

—Revelation 4:11 NASB

Contents

The Hidden Agenda

The Case for Intelligent Design

Molding the Modern Mind

The Global Search for Spirituality

Acknowledgments

Grateful appreciation is extended to all those who encouraged me to pursue the writing of this book at times of near abandonment. Special thanks to Betty Fletcher, Eileen Mason, and the faithful team at Harvest House. The selfless sacrifices of my husband, Patrick, and children, Joshua and Jonathan, were unprecedented. Abundant information from the Institute of Creation Research and John Morris's support were primary. Research contributions from Barbara Brouard, Bill Schnoeblin, Rusty Downey, Jeremiah Films' *Evolution Conspiracy*, and many others were deeply appreciated. Dorothy Miller's availability and diligent input inspired me, and the prayers of dear friends kept me sustained when the project seemed overwhelming.

> "'My grace is sufficient for you, for power is perfected in weakness.' Most gladly, therefore, I will rather boast about my weakness, that the power of Christ may dwell in me" (2 Corinthians 12:9 NASB).

—Caryl Matrisciana

I would like to thank my family—my wife, Myrna, my sons, Wade and Bryce, and my daughter, Angela—for the many sacrifices they have made which has made it possible for me to be involved in ministry. I would also like to express my gratitude to G.S. McLean; a man God has used to redirect my world view from evolution to creation, by showing me how the Word of God and the world of God both agree.

—Roger Oakland

Foreword

These are certainly interesting times in which to live. All around us we see movements and countermovements, scientific discoveries of new truth and the refutation of widely held myths, selfless commitment to causes and selfish desire for personal satisfaction. Perhaps in each decade the same observations could be made, but in the 1990's we can make them to the extreme.

In this time of polarization, we see a profound reawakening of the true church, God's people. We see a return on the part of many Christians to the God-given mandate to be salt and light in the community, after having been content to remain underground and out of sight for decades. During this time the humanists have taken over the government, the media, the schools, and the courts, but now Christians are active once again.

One of the most visible aspects of this reawakening is the modern revival of interest in creationism. Whereas in 1960 there were precious few knowledgeable people in America who held to a creationist worldview, now there are millions, with hundreds of creationist organizations and scores of good books detailing the evidence for creation. Many qualified scientists are researching and teaching, and continue to show the outstanding scientific support for creation and the weaknesses of evolution theory. Many, many people, including scientists, are leaving evolution, and new discoveries each day are fueling this exodus.

But at the same time, those who have adopted the evolutionary mindset are becoming more dogmatic and abusive than ever. Much energy is expended to insure evolution's stranglehold on education, even going so far as to censor the wealth of scientific evidence that doesn't fit with evolution. It seems evolutionists know that their model of history will not survive if competing models are allowed or even acknowledged.

Meanwhile, evolution's stepchildren—abortion, promiscuity, drugs, homosexuality—are promoted at the expense of traditional values. Even worse, the logical extensions of scientific evolutionism—cosmic consciousness, occultism, New Age thinking—are taking an unwary and uneducated public by storm, many times under the guise of science and with supposed scientific underpinnings.

Most distressing of all is the fact that during this time of polarization, while black is so clearly black and white is so clearly white, many Christians are adopting aspects of the evolutionary/occultic/New Age worldview, consistently choosing to come down on the "dark side of the gray." Christians and Christian churches everywhere are embracing evolution as God's method of creation, adapting the counseling and self-help techniques of Eastern mysticism into "Christian" counseling, utilizing New Age music in their worship services, etc. This blurring of two irreconcilable worldviews is all one-sided. The anti-Christians are not becoming more accommodating to Christian beliefs. Rather Christians are rushing to endorse, accommodate, and adopt ungodly practices and thought to their own detriment and ultimate demise. God's people everywhere need to be called back to the truth, indeed the Truth, before it is too late.

This book, *The Evolution Conspiracy: Revealing the Hidden Agenda to Deceive Mankind*, adresses this crucial issue. As the name implies, it is not so much a book about the scientific evidence (although important points are discussed) as it is a discussion of the implications of evolutionary thinking. Evolution comes across clearly as the anti-Christian way of thinking. Its evil roots are exposed, as are its truly awful fruits. A Christian who reads this book could hardly continue attempting to combine evolution and Christianity.

Others have written on such subjects before, but authors Matrisciana and Oakland add a new dimension. Their specialty, both in research and personal experience, is in the New Age arena. They know well what the term "New World Order" means.

They have a profound grasp on Eastern mysticism and recognize it in its Western garb. Their persistent sleuthing has uncovered many a connection between the occult and evolution previously undetected.

Intriguing appendixes discuss the Freemasons and the Masonic background of Charles Darwin, which played an important part in his view of reality. The fascinating lengthy section on the connection between the Grand Canyon and Hinduism illustrates how such thought infiltrates Western science and education.

Truly there is an Evolutionary Conspiracy, and it can no longer be ignored by God's people.

—John D. Morris, Ph.D.
Institute for Creation
Research

THE
EVOLUTION
CONSPIRACY

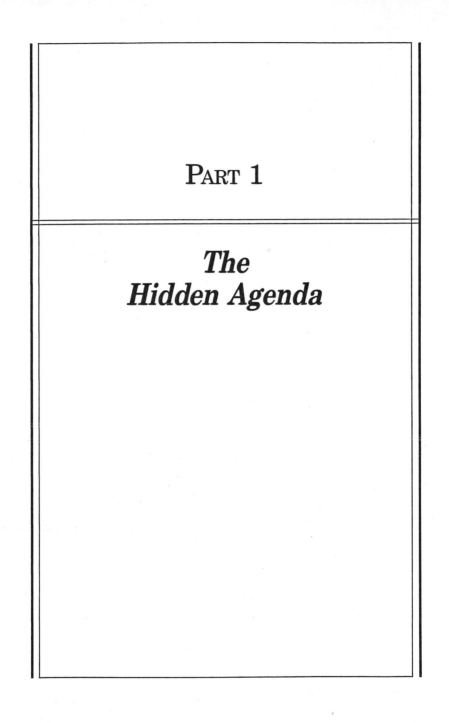

PART 1

The Hidden Agenda

CHAPTER 1

Satan's Most Lethal Weapon

Shattered marriages. Sexual promiscuity. Abortion. Euthanasia. Rampant homosexuality. Racism. Youth in rebellion. What is happening to our world? And why?

It may astonish you, but belief in the evolution of life is the source of much of our present society's confusion and waning morality. Evolutionism in all its forms has become so firmly entrenched that it now tears at the very fabric of our moral structure.

How do the "big bang" theory and other conjectures of evolutionary thinking contribute to the devastating condition of our society? What is the connection between evolutionary concepts and the state of our moral, spiritual, and physical health?

The theory of evolution holds that everything material developed as a result of natural forces, laws, and processes. In and of itself this may not sound too alarming. However, consider the spiritual implications when evolutionists make the leap from the physical to the spiritual realm. They claim that the laws of nature are constantly at work and increasing the level of man's complexity and capabilities. They say that man also has the potential to evolve in *every* aspect of his being. The "wholeness" of man—body, soul, and spirit—is supposedly also growing and becoming more spiritually advanced. Many claim that man is reaching higher levels of goodness, love, and social benevolence with each succeeding generation.

Not all those who subscribe to the evolutionary theory of biological development would acknowledge the existence of a spiritual dimension to life, let alone subscribe to the notion that the evolutionary process encompasses the spirit and soul. Nevertheless as we enter the close of this century, it is becoming more and more evident that this conjecture is gaining momentum. Without a doubt the growing advancement of the theory of biological evolution has set the stage for the next likely step in man's "progression"—the quantum leap to godhood. As Richard Greene, New Age spokesperson, explains:

> We've mastered the evolution of the physical body. We've mastered the evolution of the mind... and we're coming to a time when we're using this perfected—quasi-perfected—body, this opening and perfecting mind, to access the true perfection of the universe, which is the spiritual dimension.[1]

Growing numbers of scientists and nonscientists believe that this "spiritual evolution" is the next step in the progress of man. Yet one need only look at the world's deteriorating social conditions to see that this evolutionary hypothesis bears utterly no resemblance to reality. World press reports ought to be enough to convince even the most hardened evolutionist that man's moral and spiritual condition is becoming more debased.

Increasing crime and murder, appalling growth in satanic rituals, rampant rape and sexual abuse, intolerable crimes against children, rising numbers of abortions, and the proliferation of divorce—these surely reflect moral regression, not progression.

It is very telling to take a look back through history. The idea that ancient men were lower on the "consciousness ladder," as claimed by evolutionists, sabotages historically proven accounts of past human generations. Holy men of old were amazingly advanced in spiritual matters. They were led by divine inspiration and were intellectually leagues ahead of their counterparts today. The mental excellence of merchants and philosophers, the edifices of archeological splendor, and the advanced history of entire cultures and civilizations provide satisfactory evidence that men were originally created as men, as stated in the Bible.

Men and women created from the beginning with God-given intellect have achieved many outstanding accomplishments from the earliest times. We see no such achievements or aspirations in architecture, trade, scholarship, or any other area in the animal kingdom. One does not see the production of mathematically complex pyramids in jungles replete with apelike creatures. These are evidenced only where civilized man is known to have lived. Yet evolutionary explanations for the existence of early apelike man continue not only to mock our common sense, but to erode our morality as well.

Myriads of people are being shipwrecked in spiritually defiled waters and don't understand why they are drowning. They cling to lifeboat "Science" in the hope that its answers to the origin of life, backed up by impressive credentials and high-sounding assurances, will rescue them and provide them with the stability and meaning that they are desperately searching for. They have been hooked by false claims that the world began without supernatural intervention, and assume that this all-too-familiar theory is verifiable fact supported by scientific data.

Poison at the Roots

In replacing God's act of creation with a process of natural evolution, we are faced with the question: Have morality, truth, goodness, kindness, love, and other human values also developed from nothing?

If they have, we must accept such things as "comparative truth," "shifting absolutes," and "values clarification." And these pose serious threats to every daily decision we make. Nothing then can be based on absolutes; nothing can be determined to be right and nothing wrong if truth is seen to be forever in transition.

If, however, we believe that God, a moral Creator whose character is absolute truth, supernaturally created the universe and made man in His own image and likeness, then another picture emerges. Man inherits from Him a sense of right and wrong, truth and error. And he performs best when living in harmony with the Creator's guidelines.

A car designer precisely molds his machine and arranges its internal electronics and engineering to work best in conformity with certain strategic instructions that he has devised. For the owner of the car to deviate from the designer's intentions and instructions would be counterproductive. Guesswork or ignorance would not secure high-level performance. Only dedicated adherence to the rules laid out in the car-owner's manual guarantee the machine's successful operation.

In a similar fashion, at creation mankind was given inbuilt directives. The most important of these is the spiritual heart and instinct that God created inside man, who is able to be led by the Holy Spirit and by God's instruction manual, the Bible. This quality is unique to man alone. It is not found in animals or nature: "The Lord looketh from heaven; he beholdeth all the sons of men. . . . He fashioneth their hearts alike" (Psalm 33:13,15).

But man doesn't *want* to submit to God's guidelines. Without a Creator God man is free to develop his own moral code for his life, his home, his schools. This is the logical rebellion of evolutionary thinking.

God's law, when applied correctly, establishes man's personal and moral conduct, his family's well-being, and harmony in the ruling of the nation. All three are interwoven and dependent on God. But the individual must come to a place of personal commitment to the God of the Bible and to the authority of Scripture as truth. The first thing we are told in the Bible is "God created." Evolutionism erodes man's personal walk with God. God denied "in the beginning" brings disharmony in every other relationship in life.

Evolutionism frees man from the question of submission to God. It appeals to man's religious nature while leaving intact his intellectual pride. This explosive combination wreaked spiritual havoc with Adam and Eve (the first man and woman whom God created). And it continues to harm mankind today. The evolutionary premise is a cancerous tumor that has reached into every major circle of society and corrupted cherished values.

Calling Evolution's Hand

Although many scientists claim that mankind is scaling the evolutionary ladder, *no such evidence exists.* No scientific proof drawn from life sciences such as biology or earth sciences such as geology verifies that evolution ever occurred in the past. In fact, as we will show, today's most outstanding scientific information visibly opposes evolution.

It is interesting to note that one of the characteristics which scientific investigators claim they possess is the ability to think and observe critically. Every child in grade school is told by his or her science teacher that open-mindedness is an absolutely essential quality of a good scientist. In other words, a scientist must use critical thinking and be willing to examine all of the evidence. Uncritical thinking arises when we fail to ask for the evidence which supports all ideas and all theories.

But unfortunately, evolutionism does not always work that way. In fact, when challenges appear, the evolutionists often set themselves high upon a pedestal and proclaim their infallibility, much like a holy priesthood. The idea often projected by evolutionists is that their theory is always self-correcting and continually modifying itself— that it is a progressive truth which accommodates new facts as they are discovered. This is not true.

Is it not reasonable to question evolution if there is observable evidence which contradicts the theory? Why is it that evolutionists would rather disparage opposing views and dismiss facts which do not agree with their notions?

Creationists who claim that evolutionary teaching is based on unobservable evidence are labeled as religious fanatics who are attempting to force the "public indoctrination of a religious view."[2] Only those individuals "properly qualified within the scientific community" are capable of properly evaluating the facts, states anticreationist Willard Young in *The Fallacies of Creationism*.[3] And to really drive his point home he continues: "The obstacle the layman faces is not, in general, any lack of intelligence, but simply ignorance of the technical details of the subject. To achieve 'expert' competence in complex and difficult subjects requires many years of study and experience."[4]

Unfortunately, all too many people have fallen into the trap of accepting the opinion of so-called "authorities" and "experts" on blind faith. Certainly there are areas and concepts of science which are difficult for the nonscientific person to grasp. But one thing which everyone has the ability and the right to question is the difference between that which is fact and that which is not fact. Even the layperson has the ability to discern the difference between common sense and logic, wishful speculation and outright nonsense. History has revealed over and over again that many theories and ideas of the past have turned out to be completely erroneous, even though they were convincingly presented to the public as absolute truth. Do evolutionist scientists really have the right to declare their unchallengeable "priesthood"?

The Conspiracy Unveiled

As evolutionist scientists jealously protect their scientific "turf," Christians need to recognize that science is not alone in the battle to establish evolutionism as the *only* accepted basis for mankind's origin. There is a deadlier force at work behind such propagation.

Countless stories have been told throughout the centuries of jealous men who stole the blueprints of an invention or design from its originator. Invariably the motivation of the thief is to claim the invention as his own and keep all the glory and credit. Such plots are not unique. In fact one such scheme was acted out by the saboteur of all saboteurs—Satan himself—when in the garden of Eden he seduced Eve into undermining God's word. This wicked destroyer has not ceased his enemy tactics for a moment since. Throughout the centuries he has seduced many others—evolutionist scientists, atheists, humanist educators, and today's growing number of pagan followers—to join him in conspiring against God.

The theory of evolution is one of Satan's most lethal weapons. Like a serpent's poisonous, forked tongue, it is two-pronged: One of its consequences is earthly and the other is of eternal proportions. The first consequence is that millions of people are steered away from the worship of God by believing Satan's dishonest information about God's loving and caring character. They lose the promise of a life of spiritual satisfaction in fellowship with God in the here and now. The second damns Satan's devotees eternally. Entrapped in his malignant plot and dismissing their need for God, they deliberately choose to lose their souls and settle for permanent separation from God in the life hereafter.

Satan has set himself up in a position of equality with God. He is seeking to usurp the worship due to God the Creator. Those who believe that everything evolved out of merely natural causes are denying God's creative power and opening themselves to Satan's lies. Satan is the "father of lies" (John 8:44) and has deceived millions into believing his concoctions.

Just as he persuaded a third of the angels to believe in his power, he now passionately desires to win the affections of men despite their intuitive desire to have fellowship with God. As the prophet Jeremiah said, "The heart is deceitful above all things, and desperately wicked" (Jeremiah 17:9). Because man is easily swayed by his own self-centered desires, Satan does not have an impossible task before him in turning the hearts of men toward himself and away from God.

The Call to Arms

Considering the eternal consequences that result from the denial of God and His handiwork in creation, it is time to see just how firmly evolution has wrapped itself around our culture—and our very own lives. Caught in its grasp, we must seek to discover a way to disengage ourselves so that we can weigh evolution in the balance of truth. Is it logical? Have we accepted its ideas just because we were told they were scientific? What proof is there for evolution? And most importantly, have we let the vehemently anti-Christian values of the evolutionary premise mold our thinking?

Analyzing evolution on all its fronts, we must recognize the critical goals of the evolution/creation debate, summed up by anticreationist, science writer, and "joyous atheist" Richard Bozarth:

> The day will come when the evidence constantly accumulating around the evolutionary theory becomes so massively persuasive that even the last and most fundamental Christian warriors will have to lay down their arms and

surrender unconditionally. I believe that day will
be the end of Christianity.[5]

Satan holds no punches. His game plan is to use every
available means, in this case evolutionary supposition, to
bring people to moral chaos and eternal destruction. As
Christians in a society that has already bought unreser-
vedly into evolutionism, we have a responsibility to enter
into the fray and bring the evolution conspiracy to light.
The hearts of many depend on it.

CHAPTER 2

Seducing the Masses

Statistics assert that 70 percent of Christian children raised in evangelical homes will lose their faith by their freshman year of college.[1] That is shocking! Have we grossly underestimated the damage wreaked by 12 years of public school education that advances humanism and evolutionary theory while denying the Creator and His divine design for life?

Listen to what author Paul Blanchard writes in an article written for *The Humanist* magazine titled "Three Cheers for Our Secular State":

> Our schools may not teach Johnny to read properly, but the fact that Johnny is in school until he is 16 tends to lead towards the elimination of religious superstition. The average American child now acquires a high school education, and this militates against Adam and Eve and all other alleged myths of alleged history.[2]

And exposure to the evolutionary view isn't confined to schoolrooms. Less than a generation after its introduction into the public school system, evolutionism has successfully broken through the classroom door and honeycombed its way through mainstream Western society. Through television, films, books, activities, and fashionable fads; men, women, and children continue to be skillfully seduced. Evolutionism has become an inescapable part of our everyday lives.

Because exposure to evolutionism is so widespread and pervasive, it often passes unnoticed. Yet the thousands of bits of evolutionary thought to which we are subjected condition our thinking to a particular worldview. This worldview, if presented in its entirety, would certainly repel most of us. But taken one small dose at a time—a glance at a billboard here, a trip to a museum there—we soon become all too accepting of its bitter taste.

A brief look at some of the ways evolutionism has gained acceptance and popularity should be enough to awaken you to its inroads into your own thinking. You may begin to notice things in your everyday life that you had never thought about before in connection with a worldview that robs God of His glory and blinds man to his need of recognizing God as Creator.

Museums for the Masses

Museums have a particular responsibility to present observable evidence and facts, yet most of today's leading museums censor creationism in favor of evolutionism. Although there is a wealth of clearly observable facts to support creationist claims, museums choose to interpret the evidence to support evolutionary claims.

For example, the Smithsonian Institution, founded in Washington D.C. in 1846, is America's premier museum. It aggressively teaches evolutionism to millions of schoolchildren and adults. In addition, Smithsonian books and the *Smithsonian* magazine support evolutionism as the only viable explanation of how life originated on earth.

In a stunning pullout poster from the December 1981 *Smithsonian* magazine, the Smithsonian Institute promotes its "Tower of Time," a 27-foot mural in Dinosaur Hall at the National Museum of Natural History. The publicity says that John Gurche's painting "shows the 700-million-year span of life on Earth from single cells to modern man." This statement, presented authoritatively as fact, gives no scientific evidence to support its conclusion. Indeed, there is none.

While the film crew was filming a scene for *The Evolution Conspiracy, A Quantum Leap into the New Age* in the Smithsonian Institution, a leading paleontologist admitted off-camera that the concept of the "Tower of Time" was basically speculative and without any scientific evidence. He further admitted that none of the theories about how life originated from nonliving elements have concrete evidence to support them. Despite this, millions of visitors to the museum are led to believe that hypothetical myths such as the "Tower of Time" are scientific fact.

For museums to teach that evolutionism is the only possible explanation of the origins of life and claim that it is supported by factual scientific evidence is an outrageous condition, but one that is not restricted to museums alone. Public institutions such as libraries are also being severely impacted by increased acceptance of evolutionary theory. These depositories of knowledge ought to present a balanced presentation of facts. Yet there is a noticeable absence of books on abrupt creation. In some instances creationist books have deliberately been removed from the shelves with the explanation that they are religious and *not* scientific. One could easily argue, however, that books which attempt to explain away the existence of God using an unproven evolutionary hypothesis are more religious than scientific themselves.

Subsidized by the taxpayer's dollar, evolutionists and atheistic humanists in science and education have wrapped the religious concept of evolution in scientific costume in an attempt to disguise its very nature. Worse still, they are banding together in a designed conspiracy, intent on censoring the scientific support for creation, as we will later see.

Silent Brainwashing

Another example of the subtle evolutionary conditioning we are exposed to is illustrated by something as seemingly harmless as *National Geographic* magazine. The National Geographic Society sends its familiar yellow magazine to more than 10.8 *million* subscribers worldwide. Its readership is even larger because thousands upon thousands of these magazines are found in libraries, school rooms, doctors' offices, beauty salons, and car repair shops where many people read the same copy. With its reputation for noted researchers, extravagant scientific expeditions, stunning photography, and impeccable writing, *National Geographic* holds an unparalleled position among natural history magazines. And it is this very reputation for scientific authority that makes it so dangerous. The idea, "If it's in *National Geographic* it must be true," blinds us to the magazine's evolutionary bias and its blending of fact and fiction.

One of the most flagrant ways this mix of fact and fiction is seen is through the magazine's use of artists' conceptual drawings to illustrate evolutionary changes. To cite just one example, in 1975 some fossil footprints were found in Kenya in a layer of volcanic ash by Dr. Mary Leakey, one of the world's best-known anthropologists. Hundreds of animal tracks were found in the same location along with tracks which were believed to have been made by ancient human ancestors. Radiometric dating determined the layer of ash in which the tracks were found to be 3.5 million years old.[3] (See note below.)

In 1979 *National Geographic* reported Dr. Mary Leakey's significant fossil find to its large reading audience. Such a find was of course rewarding to the National Geographic Society, one of whose prime objectives is to promote the evolutionary worldview. Not surprisingly, Leakey's research was partially funded by the National Geographic Society.[5]

What better way to celebrate the new discovery than with a full feature article? Readers are first given a close-up picture of the actual "hominoid" (primitive man's) footprints; then a photograph showing the continuous set of footprints, comparable to those left by someone walking down a beach today. In the article, Dr. Louise Robbins of the University of North Carolina makes the comment: "They [the footprints] looked so human, so modern, to be found in tuffs so old."

---

* *Note:* Although scientists are prepared to stake their credibility on the absolute accuracy for dating volcanic materials of unknown age, it is interesting to note that when the age of formation for volcanic materials *is* known, huge discrepancies are a certainty. For example, lava rocks formed in Hawaii in 1800 and 1801 have been dated by radiometric techniques as 160 million to 3 billion years old. Other volcanic materials dated radiometrically also show erroneous results.[4] Perhaps because of some of these observed inconsistencies radiometric dating labs, before dating samples, require the researcher to fill out a form which specifies the estimated age for the sample in question.

Based on the evidence uncovered in the ash beds, *National Geographic* artist Jay H. Matternes was asked to reconstruct the scene as it may have looked 3.5 million years ago.[6] Working from the animal footprints found in the ash, Matternes painted a number of animals standing or walking around in the ash. The *animals* are exactly identical to those found today: a herd of elephants, a giraffe, an ostrich, a rabbit, and several Guinea-fowl. But drawn beside footprints which look *exactly like* those of modern humans, Matternes painted a picture of a naked, half-baboon, half-man creature carrying a club with such exquisite detail you would almost think it could walk out of the page. Is there any scientific basis for this disparity? There is not. Yet we have all seen examples of this type of subtle conditioning, and not just in *National Geographic*.

We are not saying that *National Geographic*, Jay Matternes, or Mary Leakey are purposely trying to deceive the public. But the fact remains—visual artistic illustrations are not proof that man evolved from the ape, nor are they the least bit scientific. Yet illustrations such as these have silently brainwashed millions of people. We want to make it clear: Uncritical thinking can allow someone else's conception to be your deception.

Media Madness

The media is a persuasive tool and able to effectively shift public opinion through one particularly powerful instrument—television. From children's cartoons to award-winning documentaries, the evolutionary view comes into our homes almost without our being aware. For example, the popular BBC television series "Life on Earth" shows Englishman David Attenborough walking us through seven continents and talking about some of the four million different kinds of animals and plants that "began as a life-form billions of years ago."

What this natural history series may miss is picked up from an extraterrestrial vantage point by astronomer Carl Sagan in his 13-part T.V. series, "Cosmos." The cover of his book of the same title says, *"Cosmos* is about science in its broadest human context, how science and civilization grew up together.... Sagan retraces the 15 billion years of cosmic evolution that have transformed matter into life and consciousness." Television shows such as these war against an understanding of a Creator God who made man uniquely as man from the beginning and gave him an eternal destiny that the lower life-forms do not share.

Signs of the Times

In 1986 dramatic posters and billboards strategically displayed in London advertised an intriguing traveling exhibition "The Human Story." This elaborate show was sponsored by the international computer empire IBM. Presented at the influential Commonwealth Institute museum, the no-expense-spared mood of the show was reflected in its superb publicity campaign. The campaign's eye-catching graphics depicted a lifeless male human mask being pulled off the face of an ape by the ape himself. The ape, whose piercing human eyes gave it an uncanny resemblance to modern man, stared with manipulative control at passers-by. Naturally it projected the notion that apes possess human intelligence.

The publicity blurb said, "See the exhibition that took 35 million years to put on.... It's designed to appeal to everyone from 10 upwards... and presents a synthesis of current thinking about our origins." Needless to say, the "current thinking" presented throughout reflected only the theory of evolutionists and was not balanced by other views in science today. The opinions of hundreds of creationist scientists were not aired. Many of these brilliant and impeccably educated researchers do not share the idea that animals have human intelligence or that the earth is billions of years old.

Indoctrinating the Sightseers

Evolution is also presented to millions of visitors annually at public parks and natural wonders across the country. For example, much of the visitors' information at Grand Canyon gives scientific credibility to evolutionary thesis. It perpetuates the idea that the Grand Canyon's layers were laid down over millions and millions of years and that these layers have been slowly carved out over eons of time by erosion. They do not support the alternative theory that the Grand Canyon is the product of relatively recent catastrophic flood deposition.

As we toured the visitor's center, which overlooked spectacular views of the Grand Canyon, a pleasant young park warden was happy to be our tour guide. He explained that his evolutionary view was scientific fact supported by documentation in the maps, graphs, and other information around the room. He was eager to point out that all the canyon's layers but one were laid down by water or flood activity, and he was critically hostile to the biblical explanation of a catastrophic global flood, as described in Genesis 7.

It was evident that "science" was being used to force evolutionary conditioning on the inquisitive minds of some of the three million tourists who pass through this fascinating attraction annually. (For more information on the

Grand Canyon and a look at its occultic connections, see Appendix A.)

A similar experience takes place at the fabulous La Brea Tar Pits at the Natural History Museum in Los Angeles. In the heart of America's second largest city, this attraction is one of the world's most famous fossil sites. The Tar Pits were formerly mined for natural asphalt and have yielded an incredibly rich record of more than 140 species of plants and 420 species of animals. Among the skeletons are huge mammoths, saber-toothed cats, packs of wolves, and hosts of birds—all of which became trapped and entombed. They shared their fate with everything from tiny insects to bizarre, giant ground-sloths. Among the specimens one human body was found, that of a modern-looking American Indian female said to have been murdered and concealed in the pit.

The themes of many of today's museums and amusement parks impress the public with a view of gradual deposition of life-forms over millions of years of time. The fossil record, however, can also be interpreted to have resulted from a global catastrophe which led to the sudden burial of life. All of the life-forms observed in the fossil record could have lived together at the same time and shared their sudden fate of destruction collectively.

Decade of Dinosaurs

As detailed in a later chapter, in October 1981 the National Academy of Sciences (NAS), the National Association of Biology Teachers (NABT), leading promoters of science, and numerous educators met to plan a strategy to suppress the teaching of creationism and advance the theory of evolutionism. A new enthusiasm for promoting evolutionism became evident in all areas of society.

One of the most appealing ways evolutionary theory was popularized was with the imaginative use of dinosaurs. It is one thing to acknowledge that dinosaurs existed, as the fossil record shows. It is quite another to purposely indoctrinate children and adults worldwide with the idea that dinosaurs existed *millions of years ago*, before man, and that they prove the theory of evolution.

The popularity of the dinosaur soared as prehistoric monsters were plastered on the backs of such mundane household commodities as cereal packets, milk cartons, and cookie boxes. More exquisite keepsakes like prehistoric animal commemoratives were produced by the United States Postal Service, while the American Museum of Natural History gave away full-color dinosaur wall calendars and promoted *The Land Before Time* videocassette.

The Land Before Time, a Universal Picture, was produced by two of the most financially successful and philosophically influential film directors in the world. George Lucas directed *Star Wars*, which was a blatant presentation of Eastern mysticism. Steven Spielberg, director extraodinaire, combined occultic themes in such films as *E.T.* and *Poltergeist*. These two teamed up to produce *The Land Before Time*, which was a number-one box-office hit and grossed over $46 million.

The Land Before Time not only successfully popularized Eastern philosophical concepts of evolutionism but combined them with the so-called "scientific" (evolutionist) explanation that dinosaurs roamed the earth millions of years before man ever evolved. The Bible states that man and animals were created together on day six of God's creation.

Books

Hundreds of books about dinosaurs also promote the evolutionary bias. Teachers use dinosaurs as teaching aids to promote learning skills. Educational supply stores are well-stocked with books that use dinosaurs to teach every conceivable subject. The onslaught of dinosaur-mania marches onward, unprotected, into our homes. In a lavishly expensive door-to-door promotional, Britannica Home Library Service of Chicago "invites your child to travel millions of years back in time...." It promises as a free introductory offer the first marvelous book of a finely illustrated 23-volume series, "The World of Dinosaurs." The impressive promotion, packaged in an enticing, full-color, dinosaur-crammed envelope reads, "Introduce your child to all the wonder, excitement and knowledge of dinosaurs... [which] actually lived—in fact, dominated the earth—from over 200 million to 60 million years ago when they mysteriously disappeared...." Unsuspecting parents often overlook the spiritual implications of evolutionism as they assist their children to progress along the road of "scientific" education.

Summer Fun

Frustrated parents seeking to survive spring and summer school breaks are willing to try any adventure to liven up bored children. One suggestion comes from a children's book written by paleontologist Niles Eldredge, *The Fossil Factory: A Kid's Guide to Digging up Dinosaurs, Exploring Evolution and Finding Fossils*. It lists where fossils can be found both in the ground and in museums, and pushes evolution as fact, not a possible alternate theory.

Another suggestion comes from the Pacific Science Center, Seattle, Washington ("where science isn't a subject, it's an experience," says the brochure). With the incentive "Discover a New Cure for Boredom," a lively variety of science activities are challengingly presented. "Use your hands... touch, explore, see and learn about the world we live in" invites the museum. What could be better? Yet in the midst of all the opportunities, evolution beckons, "Transport yourself back 140 million years to Dinosaurs: A journey through time." One can only beg the question, is it not possible to enjoy pure science without the pseudo-science or philosophy of evolution being added?

Enticing Attractions

Knott's Berry Farm, Anaheim, California, privately owned and operated by the Knott family, is advertised "as one of the most popular and famous theme parks in the world." In the summer it attracts from 20,000 to 30,000 visitors *each day* and its 165 rides, shows, and attractions, set on 150 acres, are specifically geared to please older adults and children.

Knott's prides itself in "the relative strength of [its] capacity as an educational resource" and wishes "to be well-woven within the educational fabric of our community." It offers an appealing "Adventures in Education" program which promotes six exciting science adventures from "Minerals of the Earth" to "Marine Mammals of America." Promoted as "edu-tainment," "The New Age of Dinosaurs" is one of the educational presentations that furthers the cause of evolution.

It took $7 million to build and advertise Knott's grandiose Kingdom of Dinosaurs. As public interest in dinosaurs boomed, Knott's caught the wave and through this impressive gimmick beat their amusement-park competitor Disneyland in gate sales. Twelve to fifteen people squeeze into a car that takes them back "200 million years" into "Professor Wells' laboratory and through his Time Machine, every 7 minutes from 9 A.M. to midnight."

That's a lot of people to be deluged with the evolutionary premise and history of dinosaurs. And as you proceed out of the exhibition area a huge, colorful wall mural pictorially depicts the supposed eons from first forms of life to today's Homo sapiens.

As if that were not enough, on-site paleontologists prepare fossils and share evolutionary perspectives with the interested public at the exit to the exhibit. They are available to answer questions, and those we talked to were openly critical of creationist views. They were especially condemning of the creationist view that today's fossil record was caused by a catastrophic global flood. Instead they explained that the fossil record is the result of local flash floods from ancient Egypt to England to Canada, which took place over millions of years.

Selling Power

The power of dinosaurs to attract attention has become so well-recognized that many companies feature them in their advertising. ITI uses a colorful advertisement with an imposing giant of a dinosaur above copy that reads, "History is full of giants who couldn't adapt." The company maintains that they "offer you a whole new world of innovative operator services, while the giant (AT&T) continues to lumber along.... it's the smarter, quicker guy that prevails. That's how evolution works."

Manipulating people into a particular way of thinking is nothing new. It's a practice as old as the deceptive ways of Satan himself. As we have seen, millions upon millions of people are being captivated by evolutionary thinking, perhaps without consciously realizing what is happening. We'll soon see how this fits with biblical prophecy and with Satan's plan to shape the moral, intellectual, and political future of the world.

CHAPTER 3

Changing the Value of Human Life

A s we continue into the last decade of this century, it is evident that something is tragically amiss in our society's moral structure. A recent study reports that "about 600,000 teenagers in the U.S. will become pregnant annually—23,000 aged 14 or younger. More than 40 percent of pregnancies in the 15- to 19-year-olds will be aborted and 60 percent of these girls under 15."[1]

And consider these statistics:

- The United States has a rape rate that is 13 times higher than Britain, 4 times higher than Germany, and 20 times higher than Japan.
- In New York City, Mayor David Dinkins appointed three lesbian judges in his first four judicial appointments.
- Stanford University trustees approved a policy that gives homosexual and unmarried couples the same rights as legally married couples to campus housing and university services.[2]

What do any of these statistics have to do with evolutionism? They reveal the changing attitudes of a culture in which people are choosing to direct the course of their own lives without regard to the design of their Creator. Ignoring the clear direction of the Bible and denying the witness of creation, society is now rolling down the steep embankment of moral decline.

Denying God's Handiwork

Ask the average person who admits to the existence of God how he "knows" that there is a God and he'll probably shrug his shoulders and answer, "I just know." Yet the Bible explains why everyone "knows" of God's existence. Psalm 19:1 says, "The heavens declare the glory of God; and the firmament sheweth His handiwork."

The first chapter of the book of Romans is familiar to many. But let's look with fresh eyes at a passage that provides keen insight into evolution and morality from God's perspective:

> For since the creation of the world His invisible attributes, His eternal power and divine nature, have been clearly seen, being understood through what has been made, so that they [people] are without excuse. For even though they knew God, they did not honor Him as God, or give thanks; but they became futile in their speculations, and their foolish heart was darkened. Professing to be wise, they became fools, and exchanged the glory of the incorruptible God for an image in the form of corruptible man and of birds and four-footed animals and crawling animals.... They exchanged the truth of God for a lie, and worshiped and served the creature rather than the Creator (Romans 1:20-25 NASB).

In this passage we see God's clear analysis of the evolutionist's hardness of heart. He knows that God exists because God's divine nature is clearly seen in creation, yet he does not want to give God honor where honor is due. He insists that animals, reptiles, and man are able to sustain life outside of God's intervention. And for such thoughts of ingratitude God gives the evolutionist over to the foolish speculations of his heart: "But my people would not hearken to my voice . . . so I gave them up unto their own hearts' lust: and they walked in their own counsels. Oh that my people had hearkened unto me . . ." (Psalm 81:11-13).

All of nature calls us to believe that God deliberately created the world and the universe. According to the Bible we are to believe that He created each species of plant and animal, and ultimately man. He did so abruptly, uniquely, and intentionally (Genesis 1,2). We are also to believe that in His wisdom, He established laws for human behavior.

In contrast, evolutionism contests God, His creative power, His unique plan and purpose for man, His time span (the design of time and the length of His days), His morality, and His judgments. (See the Recommended Reading list at the back of this book for material that goes into more detail on these important discussions.)

Christians and the Moral Landslide

Today's moral deterioration is not confined to non-Christians. Countless Christians are allowing the claims of evolution to tamper with the moorings of their faith. Their belief is being destroyed by atheists, humanistic scientists, evolutionary thinkers, and incredibly even by those who identify themselves with Christianity. Through evolutionary indoctrination, these various parties wage war against the testimony of nature and the legitimacy and authority of the Christian's soul-book, the Bible. In so doing, they cultivate seeds of confusion and rebellion.

First Timothy 4 starts out with this warning: "But the Spirit explicitly says that in later times some will fall away from the faith, paying attention to deceitful spirits and doctrines of demons" (verse 7 NASB). The verses that follow point to a decline in morality being the result of wrong teaching. Twice they mention God's authority as the Creator of all.

This text is addressed to men and women who knew of God as their Creator but were being won away from His morality by the desires and lusts of their flesh. This frighteningly reflects the condition of today's church. *Time* magazine recently ran a feature article on the intense controversies that Christian churches are facing with respect to moral issues such as homosexuality and sexual relations outside of marriage. The article explains that "the tenet that sex should be confined to marriage is an age-old one inherited from Judaism."[3] It goes on to say that this belief is under assault "because of the pressures of modern reality: the sexual precocity of young Americans, the large number of divorced or unmarried adults who have active sex lives, and the growing strength of the gay-rights movement."

These pressures, combined with dwindling church attendance and opposition from feminist groups that label Christianity "patriarchal" (as do growing numbers of witches, pagans, and nature worshipers, who see "Mother Earth" as a goddess and God as a female power), are causing churches to change the meaning of the Bible to comply with social behavior and preferences.

The Bible's remedy, however, lies in the opposite direction—in the believer returning to original faith in the

Creator and denying the seductive call of "worldly fables" (1 Timothy 4:7 NASB).

Paul ends his letter to Timothy, "Guard what has been entrusted to you, avoiding worldly and empty chatter and the opposing arguments of what is falsely called 'knowledge' [King James "science"]—which some have professed and thus gone astray from the faith" (1 Timothy 6:20,21 NASB).

Paul's salient point is that belief in any of the many worldly speculations and "opposing arguments" to the Word of God, one of which would certainly be evolution, will result in an apostasy. This "falling away" from the faith will be evidenced by a decline of morality.

And this is exactly what is happening. The result is an avalanching away from biblical tenets, a serious moral landslide bolstered by the weak crutch of humanism based on evolution.

The effects of this decline, within the church and without, are causing the foundations of our society to crumble. This is clearly seen in the shifting nature of our country's legal system.

Absolutely No Absolutes

The writers of the Constitution knew the importance of a Bible-based religion. It restrains man's sin nature and maintains virtue. In his farewell address George Washington said, "Reason and experience both forbid us to conclude that national morality can prevail in exclusion of religious principle."

John Adams, when he was the U.S. ambassador to France, observed that "the United States Constitution was made only for a moral and religious people. It is wholly inadequate for the government of any other."[4]

The Constitution was designed on the principle (derived from English legal tradition) that certain laws are fixed and absolute. These foundational laws are established by God and communicated to man for application to his legal system.

Without a foundation of biblical values, and people who are committed to upholding them, it is fair to say that there is no recognition of "absolute" or "universal" laws. Rather laws are subject to change, just as everything else in the evolutionary scheme is subject to change.

Because of this, today's law has deviated and is now based on the theory of evolution. This new view is called legal positivism, and it insists that there are no divine and fixed absolutes. Instead of being God-inspired, laws are now based on man's authority, and the highest human authority who has the power will enforce their application. Such a concept is permissible since man evolves, our society evolves, and our legal system evolves. Therefore the Constitution must evolve too.[5]

This evolutionary concept allows for shifting legal explanations with the progress of time. Just before his election, Woodrow Wilson, a former president of the United States, said, "All we progressives ask or desire is permission to interpret the Constitution according to the Darwinian principle of evolution."[6]

Justice Brennan, who redefined the "religious" viewpoint at the Louisiana "Creation Law" trial in 1987, openly stated that he wanted the Constitution to be interpreted according to an "evolutionary principle," which he said is the "true interpretive genius of the text." This is an overt reversal of the original intent of the Constitution, which was based on standards and truths consistent with the Word of God.

The result of a shift toward legal positivism is that any type of judgment from human judiciary becomes confused and contradictory. If man is simply an evolving animal, much of the behavior which is identified as sinful and degenerate by divine law is excusable. Imprisonment or remedial punishment makes no sense. God's final judgment of spiritual hell in this context would be considered barbaric—certainly not an appropriately progressive solution.

Psychologists and psychiatrists have redefined "sin," calling it "low self-esteem." This condition, they claim, is what drives people to emotional mayhem. The solution is to spend billions of tax dollars in public school programs to encourage better self-esteem through the use of imagination, visualization, hypnosis, and other altered mental states. These techniques are rooted in paganism founded on evolutionism. The biblical solution, however, is to recognize sin for what it is, repent, and seek God's cleansing.

Beyond Human Dignity

One of the effects of legal positivism has been the steady devaluing of human life. The biblical view that man was created in the image of God is what gives life dignity. It also gives man certain God-given human rights. On the other hand, humanists who demand human rights based on evolutionary principles don't actually have any such "human rights" implicit in their philosophical framework. The *Roe v. Wade* decision, which legalized abortion, amply illustrates this.

The Fourteenth Amendment clearly stipulates "that no state shall deprive any person of life, liberty, or property without due process of law." Rather than support the idea that abortion in fact "deprives life," the Supreme Court took the phrase "liberty" to include a "right of privacy." In this victory for humanists the Court ruled that a mother had the "right of privacy," meaning the right to make decisions concerning her life, and the right to terminate an unwanted pregnancy.

Embryos, zygotes, or fetuses are appropriate names in medical terms. But they do not subtract from the baby's personhood in God's eyes. In Psalm 51:5 David says, "Behold, I was shapen in iniquity; and in sin did my mother conceive me." This means that unborn David in the womb was in the same sin-state as Adam's children in Genesis 5:3. All were born in their parents' likeness, not God's, with a sin nature. An unborn baby must be a person to have a sin nature.

Today, through innovative camera processes, modern man can view the miraculous process that David spoke about. Started at the moment of conception, in marvelous tiny detail, video film reveals new life developing inside the womb. Such visions enable the spectator to choose to believe in the wonder David spoke about, or to view with cynicism the evolution of a meaningless blob of tissue.

One of the leading advocates of legal positivism and a noted evolutionist was Supreme Court Justice Oliver Wendell Holmes. In one of his speeches he said, "I see no reason to attribute to man any significance above that of an ape or other being."[7]

It's true! Evolutionism determines that man is of little value. He is likened to amoebas, fish, and apelike creatures. Columnist Joseph Sobran explains that many people "suppose that the fetus is in the early stages of development a 'lower' form of life, and this is probably what they mean when they say it isn't 'fully human.'"[8]

One has little hesitation about killing a fish, and sadly the same idea has dulled man's conscience in regard to his own offspring. In a recent survey, it was reported that almost two million unborn children were aborted in one year in the United States and Canada. That adds up to more deaths than were taken by cancer, heart disease, and automobile accidents combined.

"So the abortion debate has its roots in two alternative ways of imagining the unborn," Sobran continues. "Our civilization, until recently, agreed in imagining the unborn child on the pattern of the Incarnation, which maximizes his dignity; but many people now imagine him on the pattern of evolution, as popularly understood, which minimizes his dignity."[9]

Death Rites

Now that the floodgates are open, further discussion proposes legitimizing other areas of killing. Infanticide. Euthanasia. Abortion of babies born under so-called repugnant conditions—rape, incest, ill-health of the mother, or the threat of severe disabilities. All such considerations lessen the value of some lives in comparison to others. To imply that certain circumstances are so deplorable that a child must give its life as compensation is to violate the sanctity of human life.

Pro-life speaker Mary Senander's article in the *Star Tribune* addresses this serious concern:

> There are many negative acts that may result in pregnancy—crack, or too much booze, loveless marriages or one-night stands—but rape and incest currently fan the hottest fires. . . . If National Right to Life Committee (NRLC) and its affiliate, Minnesota Citizens Concerned for Life (MCCL) suggest that conceived-but-not-yet-born

humans can be killed because of potential life-threatening disabilities, what about those already among us who have actual life-threatening disabilities? The "personhood" issue is increasingly raised in euthanasia-related debates to justify the withholding of food and fluids from severely disabled humans who are, according to some, not dying quickly enough. It is inconsistent to oppose euthanasia while approving certain abortions. NRLC's and MCCL's acquiescence to fetal euthanasia sends a mixed (and deadly) message to people with handicaps and their families; better never born than born disabled.[10]

Within the premise of man's evolution from animal, it is possible to rationalize infanticide (the killing of a baby after birth) and consider it an honorable act of decency. Barbara Burke writes: "Among some animal species, then, infant killing appears to be a natural practice. Could it be natural for humans, too, a trait inherited from our primate ancestors.... Charles Darwin [considered the founding father of evolutionism] noted in *The Descent Of Man* that infanticide has been 'probably the most important of all checks' on population growth throughout most of history."[11]

In a similar vein, many people consider it kinder to shoot a hurt animal than let it continue in pain. Seeing ourselves as evolved animals legitimizes "pulling the plug" on an infirm patient. The health care worker ordered by the courts to remove the tube or preside over the death of a sick person by starvation and dehydration becomes the executioner, in direct conflict with his or her calling to care for the sick. In the future, the unwillingness of the health care worker to perform such an act could conceivably result in a jail sentence or expulsion from the medical profession.

If it is considered acceptable to put "an old horse (man's cousin somewhere along the evolutionary path) out to pasture," surely human euthanasia could be considered equally noble. Deciding to extinguish or prolong life based on the performance of a person could justify the death of any person seen to be less than normal or unable to contribute whatever society deems beneficial.

God considers each life precious. The quality of human life doesn't diminish its value in God's eyes, and it is not the decisive factor in determining whether to sustain or eliminate someone's physical existence. From God's perspective euthanasia, suicide, infanticide, and abortion constitute unjustifiable destruction and are not morally permissible. Humanistic evolutionism violates God's ordinances, which give us stewardship over human life, not dominion.

Caring for the elderly, less fortunate, weak, and infirm are Christian duties encouraged in the Scriptures:

> We then that are strong ought to bear the infirmities of the weak, and not to please ourselves (Romans 15:1).

> Comfort the feebleminded, support the weak, be patient toward all men. See that none render evil for evil unto any man; but ever follow that which is good (1 Thessalonians 5:14,15).

The elderly have a special purpose in life and in God's view. Psalm 92:14 says that "they shall still bring forth fruit in old age." Man's mission on earth is to bring people into knowledge of God's kingdom, and that joyful responsibility can be accomplished at any age and through any circumstance. To exterminate whatever man deems as weaknesses either in the infirm, the unborn, the catastrophically ill, or the aged is to place man and his plan above God's destiny.

Throughout the Bible we see people of God enduring burdensome situations of ill health, loss of possessions, physical assault, and emotional turmoil. Yet they believed God to be in control of all of life's circumstances and had the assurance that all things work together for good to accomplish His purposes through His strength.

Playing God

As our technological capabilities have increased, other areas of critical concern have arisen. Biotechnology is in essence a field of experimentation on infirm humans using vital parts of already-dead human bodies. That this field of technology should be dependent on unbiblical precedents is indeed an area of moral debate. Aborted fetuses or cells from various organs of killed babies are vital in surgery for human grafting in kidney transplants, diabetes, and Parkinson's disease.

Another controversial topic—in vitro fertilization of the human ovum to produce "test tube babies"—has opened a legal hornet's nest. Arbitrarily deciding who parents whatpreference-of-genes is nothing short of playing God in the destiny of life.

John White, retired psychiatrist and author, says:

> I think these researchers [biological engineers] are slipping into playing God. All research arises out of a view of the universe, and secular doctors view matter as a thing in itself without

reference to God. A scientist either takes the role of a magician or prophet. The prophet hears the word and obeys it. The power and authority of the prophet spring from his desire to be obedient to God.

The magician, on the other hand, desires power in and of itself and wants God's power to do miracles. He may not call it God's power, but he lusts to play a God-like role. This magician's mentality is almost universal in scientific research.[12]

Evolution's Sacred Cows

Another result of evolutionary thinking is the idea that all matter, whether man or animal, has the same value. God says differently. Ecclesiastes 3:21 says, "Who knoweth the spirit of man that goeth upward, and the spirit of the beast that goeth downward to the earth?"

If man believes that animals are his next-of-kin, he may logically seek to protect them over and above his fellow-humans. This is why animal rights campaigns, started in the 1960's, remain well-ingrained in the 1990's environmental protection movement. Concerned organizations claim that the lives of animals, which are being used in medical experimentation to save human lives, are being unnecessarily and cruelly abused.

Laboratories involved in such important research are often bombed and sabotaged by animal lovers. The protests of such activists can be seen in "save the whale" demonstrations and in media stories which wage war against abusive environmental practices. But where are these voices when thousands of human lives are butchered at abortion clinics? They campaign for the rights of endangered animals, unborn animals, and nature, giving them priority over the rights of unborn humans.

Hinduism, India's predominant religious belief, is based on this same evolutionary rationale. In India rats are sacred and given care above humans (the same thing is happening in California where concern over a possibly endangered species of rat is being given priority over the housing needs of humans). And cows, Hinduism claims, are higher on the evolutionary ladder than many Indian humans. Cows are revered as gods while newborn girls are slaughtered because they are not born males. Living widows are burned with their husbands' corpses at the pyre because it is believed that the lives of females are not of as much value as males. (See note below.)

The Indian "untouchable" male, the lowest of the four (sometimes classified as five) religious Hindu castes, is not worth much either. Like the lepers of old, and today's dogs on Indian streets, the "untouchable" is restricted to life on the outskirts of the village. If his shadow were to cross that of a higher caste even today, it would be considered acceptable to kill him.

If man believes in higher and lower castes, order, or stages of humankind, as Charles Darwin postulated in his book *The Descent of Man*, eliminating the "savage races" (Darwin's classification of what he considered to be inferior races) is justified. Such conflicts fall under the edicts of evolution's laws of "natural selection," also called "the survival of the fittest."

---

* *Note:* Caryl Matrisciana was born in India and lived there for 20 years. She has written about her life there in *Gods of the New Age*.

This outrageously racist and savage doctrine combined with its political implications, was played out to its fullest cruelty by Darwin's admirer Adolf Hitler. Dr. Henry Morris states, "Darwin's idea that evolution means 'the preservation of favored races in the struggle for life' eventually led to Nazism and the Jewish holocaust. . . . The Nazi leaders certainly used evolutionary theory to provide scientific justification for their barbaric actions."[13]

In his book *Sedimentary Petrology and Biologic Evolution*, Kenneth J. Hsu, a Chinese geologist, says that "in the biological theory of Darwin, Hitler found his most powerful weapon against traditional values."[14]

As Arthur Keith, in his book *Evolution and Ethics*, states, "The ways of national evolution, both in the past and in the present, are cruel, brutal, ruthless and without mercy . . . the law of Christ is incompatible with the law of evolution."[15]

The philosophy of evolution taken to its logical conclusion destroys the sanctity of life and can only bring out the worst in man. In becoming the captain of his own destiny, the evolutionist is able to justify even the most morally reprehensible behavior. And the victims of such behavior are the very people who are least able to defend themselves in the midst of moral chaos.

CHAPTER 4

Preparation for Delusion

The consequences of evolutionary thinking are clear: a hardening of the heart toward God and a decline in morality. But why has a theory that violates values which much of civilization has held dear for thousands of years been embraced so rapidly in the past few centuries? Is it only that the advances of modern science seem to "prove" evolution? Or is there a hidden agenda at work, a game plan which fits the designs of Satan to deceive mankind in the last days, and so hold him captive for eternity?

Far from being a purely scientific pursuit, evolution's history over the past 200 years shows that it has been a means to a variety of social, political, and religious ends. The motives and goals of significant people and events can give valuable insight into why evolutionary thinking has progressed so far, and into the conspiracy at work to shape the minds of people to an evolutionary worldview.

The French Connection

Through the Middle Ages, belief in a Creator God was

the normal course of reasoning among people in Judeo-Christian cultures. The first major challenge to scriptural revelation occurred in the country of France in the 1700's.

During the 1770's, thousands of lives were lost in a bloody uprising known as the French Revolution. At that time France's corrupt king and equally corrupt church were swept away from their positions of authority. The new socialist state was proclaimed a republic. During this violent process France philosophically rejected the rulership of God, whom their king and church had so poorly represented, and the revolutionaries elected a committee of godless men to govern them by human reason.[1]

In 1793 the French Legislative Assembly unanimously renounced the belief in and worship of a deity. This was followed shortly afterward by the public burning of the Bible.[2] Almost overnight, France turned from Roman Catholicism to atheism. The few people in the country who continued to defend the Bible were sent into exile or worse, lost their lives. A generation of idealists emerged, philosophers who believed that human reason alone offered the pathway to a perfect future.

The concepts which led to the French Revolution were inspired by two famous French philosophers, Rene Descartes and Jean Jacques Rousseau. Descartes (1596-1650) has often been called the father of modern philosophy. In his book *Discourse on Method*, published in 1637, he proposed that the universe was a mechanism governed by mathematical laws. Because these laws operated by nature, he asserted that divine intervention was unnecessary, and that man did not possess a free will. This mindset reduced mankind to a mere machine governed by mathematical equations. It established a foundation for intellectuals who were looking for a way to explain human nature, society, and government without acknowledging a Creator God.[3]

Rousseau (1712-1778), was born into a Protestant home, converted to Roman Catholicism, and finally renounced Christianity completely. He denied the biblical fall of man, explaining instead that man was born basically good and had been corrupted by society.[4] He challenged biblical miracles and relegated God to the role of an absentee landlord. In 1762 Rousseau wrote *The Social Contract*, a book which put forward a radical and secular view of government based on the general will of the people rather than on laws appointed by God. This philosophy, more than any other, paved the way for the French Revolution.

England's Quiet Struggle

While France was rebelling against corruption in its church-state government, England at the end of the eighteenth century presented a much less volatile picture. The Industrial Revolution, which began in the 1700's, had made England one of the greatest nations on earth. In this atmosphere new ideas were free to develop, unthwarted by violence or bloodshed.

Religiously, Britain contrasted sharply with France. Britain was a Protestant country, having divorced itself from Catholicism in the early 1500's. Beginning in the eighteenth century and continuing throughout the nineteenth century, the majority of British people believed that the Bible was true, and had no reason to doubt its miracles—including the creation account in Genesis.[5]

The church played a major role in British society during this period of history. Religion and history were considered essential social foundations for the order and stability of society.[6] Many people applauded poet laureate Robert

Southey when he wrote in 1829, "Nothing is more certain than that religion is the basis upon which civil government rests. And it is necessary that this religion be established for the security of the state, and for the welfare of the people."[7]

In those days, attacks on religion and the church were not only blasphemous and immoral, but socially dangerous as well. Yet by the late 1700's, seeds of discontent within the British intellectual community were beginning to take root. One group of heretical thinkers belonged to an organization called the Lunar Society of Birmingham, which met once a month at the time of the full moon. This aristocratic group of men sought social change and the advancement of a secular society. Active from 1764 to 1800, the group never included more than 14 members. These members were, however, some of the most influential men in England, and their primary intention was to remove the church from a position of power in Great Britain.[8]

The Lunar Society recognized the Bible as the greatest single obstacle to the achievement of its socialistic aims. It concluded that generating disbelief in the Bible would be the most effective way of changing public opinion. But casting doubt on such beloved doctrines as the virgin birth of Jesus Christ or the resurrection would have been too shocking to the culture of that day. Instead, the Lunar Society chose to discredit the biblical accounts of the creation and the flood.[9]

The founder of the Lunar Society was a man named Erasmus Darwin (1731-1802), grandfather of Charles Darwin. Erasmus Darwin's contribution to the emerging view of evolution was a two-volume work written in 1794-96 called the *Zoonomia*. Although Charles Darwin was born seven years after his grandfather died, the ideas of Erasmus Darwin deeply influenced his life. *Zoonomia* expressed the essence of the theory that his grandson announced to the world five decades later.[10]

New Ideas About Earth's Age

Another challenge to the biblical view of creation was put forward by James Hutton (1726-1797). Although Hutton had a Quaker background, he eventually rejected the belief in a literal worldwide flood. He argued that the earth's history could best be explained by examining the earth's layers rather than accepting the validity of questionable Jewish records.[11]

Hutton proposed that the earth had been molded not by sudden violent events, but by slow and gradual processes—the same processes that can be observed in the world today. This theory became known as "uniformitarianism."

Today, Hutton's proposal is considered a turning point in history. The introduction to one university biology textbook summarizes the importance of Hutton's ideas: "It was geologists more than biologists who paved the way for evolutionary theory."

Hutton's theory of uniformitarianism began to bring about several changes in thinking:

First, it implied that the earth has a living history and a long one. This was a new idea. Christian theologians, by counting the successive generations since Adam (as recorded in the Bible), had calculated the maximum age of the earth at about six thousand years. Six thousand years is not enough time for such major evolutionary changes as the formation of new species to take place. Up to this time this view had precluded any explanations about the origin of life that required long periods of time.

Second, the theory of uniformitarianism stated that change is the normal course of events. This went against the generally held view that the earth was a relatively stable system interrupted by an occasional catastrophic events such as floods.

Third, although this was never explicit, uniformitarianism suggested that there might be interpretations of the Bible other than the literal one.[12]

Hutton's was the first prominent scientific voice that not only promoted a humanist view of the origin and history of earth, but boldly undermined the authenticity of the Bible. He expanded the accepted biblical time frame for the age of the earth and refuted the biblical account of a global flood.

Evolutionary Sabotage

Charles Lyell (1797-1875), who is remembered for his significant contributions to the development of uniformitarian geology, was born the year James Hutton died. He was a lawyer, a politician, an amateur geologist, and the author of *The Principles of Geology* (1830-33).

There is good reason to believe that Lyell's proposals may not have been based entirely on openminded scientific observation. In 1826, at the age of 29 and with no formal science background, he was elected a fellow of the Royal Society, an elitist institution founded by the Lunar Society.[13] Lyell had two qualities which were of interest to the Royal Society: He was able to write clearly, and he had a keen interest in evolutionary geology.[14]

Francis Hitchings, author of the *World Atlas of Mysteries* considers Lyell's motives:

> It was as much for political reasons as scientific reasons that the new theory of uniformitarianism grew up to challenge the biblical theory of Creation. If the Bible told the truth, there was no way of peacefully challenging the monarchy in Britain, for sovereignty was supposed to descend from God to the King; but if the Bible could be shown to be inaccurate, particularly in respect to the key event of the Deluge, then the whole philosophical foundation on which the monarchy based its power would be shattered. That at any rate was the reasoning of a group of Whig lawyers and MP's, one of whom was Charles Lyell, who published his *Principles of Geology*.[15]

Forty years after the publication of *The Principles of Geology*, Charles Darwin commented on Lyell's effectiveness in casting doubt on the Bible. Passages like the one that follows, written by Darwin about Lyell, have not been generally made available to the public. They are part of a vast body of correspondence which remains to this day unpublished and confined to the archives of Cambridge University Library.[16] It has not been published because it reveals the motives behind the founding fathers of evolution. Darwin says:

> Lyell is most firmly convinced that he has shaken the faith in the Deluge far more efficiently by never having said a word against the Bible than if he had acted otherwise. . . . I have

> read lately Morley's *Life of Voltaire* and he insists
> strongly that direct attacks against Christianity
> produce little permanent effect; real good seems
> only to follow slow and silent side attacks.[17]

Center Stage

Clearly towering above all others, Charles Darwin (1809-1882) stands in most people's minds as the father of evolution. Indeed, the terms Darwinism and evolution have become relatively synonymous.

Darwin was born into a family of means and intellectual distinction. As a child, young Charles showed no signs of having exceptional abilities. School in general failed to capture his interest. His father, Robert, was a successful physician and Charles was initially persuaded to study medicine at Edinburgh. The subject matter, however, did not appeal to him, and after two years he moved on to Christ's College in Cambridge and began to prepare for a life in the ministry. Though never known as a diligent student, he nevertheless had a deep interest for natural history.

Darwin graduated from seminary in 1831. At the age of 22 he was prepared to take the title of the Reverend Charles Darwin to a small Anglican country church, close to the natural world that he loved. But rather than finding a position as preacher of the Bible, he instead accepted an invitation to become a naturalist aboard the *HMS Beagle*, a ship which traveled around the world. The course of his life was changed forever.

The momentous voyage, which began in December of 1831, transformed Darwin's thinking. He describes his original point of view:

I did not then in the least doubt the strict and literal truth of every word in the Bible.[18]

Whilst on board the Beagle I was quite orthodox, and I remember being heartily laughed at by several of the officers for quoting the Bible as an unanswerable authority on some point of morality.[19]

How were Darwin's religious views so drastically changed? Some claim it was the geological observations he made while traveling around the world that caused him to doubt the authenticity of the Bible.[20] Others suggest that Lyell's *Principles of Geology*, which he read during the voyage, exerted a powerful influence on his thinking as the journey progressed.[21] Whatever the case, he rapidly moved away from a belief in fundamental Christianity to agnosticism. By the late 1830's he had completely abandoned his original Christian faith.

It has often been rumored that during the latter part of his life, Darwin was concerned about the way his theory had undermined the Christian faith. However, his autobiography leaves little room for speculation regarding the motives behind his work. Describing the two years of his life following the return of the *Beagle* to England, Darwin made the following statement:

I was led to think much about religion. But I had gradually come by this time, to see that the Old Testament from its manifestly false history of the world, with the Tower of Babel, the rainbow as a sign, etc. and from attributing to God the feelings of a revengeful tyrant, was no more to be trusted than the sacred book of the Hindoos, or the beliefs of any barbarian.[22]

Another insight into Darwin's thinking is reflected in his involvement with Freemasonry, an occultic philosophy that is incompatible with basic biblical tenets. In 1867 he was made a Knight of the Prussian Order, "Pour le Merite." This was considered a weighty achievement in Freemason circles.

A Prussian Knight is known to have reached the twenty-first degree of the Scottish Rite. In Darwin's day, to be a twenty-first degree Mason was no mean feat. Such a step would have required hours and hours of ritual memorization and fanatical commitment (today there is less memorization and less prestige associated with the degree).

Darwin's quest for an alternative to creation fits perfectly into the Freemason's agenda to destroy the biblical account of creation. Freemasonry does not believe in the God of the Bible who could create something out of nothing. Instead the Freemason's god is called "the Architect of the Universe." And, true to its definition, an architect must start with existing materials in order to build. In order to be a committed Freemason one has to compromise and ultimately estrange oneself from Christian ideology, which Charles Darwin eventually did. (For a fuller discussion of Freemasonry and Darwin's occultic connections, see Appendix B.)

Earthshaking Books

In his works, Charles Darwin offered solutions to two burning questions of his day: What precisely are the causal origins of living things? And, Where did human beings come from? Darwin's thesis was based on the theory that organisms are what they are because of a process bound by natural law. He claimed that all living things have ascended through many generations, generally being modified from a few initial primitive forms.

Darwin's ideas were publicly put forward in two major books. His first, *On the Origin of Species*, was published in 1859, subtitled *By Means of Natural Selection or the Preservation of Favoured Races in the Struggle for Life*. The second, published in 1871, was called *The Descent of Man, and Selection in Relation to Sex*. Both of these books cast deep doubt upon formerly cherished Christian beliefs, opening the door to new horizons of thought.

With these two strokes, Charles Darwin gave modern science a rational and revolutionary way of thinking about the universe and everything in it. Without question, the arrival of Darwin's books changed the world.

Making Agnosticism Respectable

It was not long before Darwin's theory on the origin and development of life became well known. Soon intellectuals applied the concept of biological evolution to their own theories about social evolution. A number of new philosophies began to emerge based on Darwinian theory. These ideas burst rapidly on the scene, carrying implications which made agnosticism and atheism respectable.

Karl Marx, who was living in London at the time and developing his own manuscript called *Das Kapital*, was delighted to find a scientific rationale in Darwin's theory of evolution that gave validation to his own new philosophy. Marx compared the struggle for survival among organisms to the struggle for power among social classes. He and other humanists of the day believed the individual, not God, was the highest being. Darwinian theory combined with Marxist ideology formed the cornerstone of the "superman" doctrine—the survival of the fittest or the duty of the strong to trample the weak.

Marx admired Darwin, and the two corresponded. Today, in Darwin's library outside of London, a token of Marx's appreciation can be seen in an inscription from Marx to Darwin in Darwin's complimentary copy of *Das Kapital*. Marx had attempted to dedicate this great atheistic work to Darwin, but Darwin refused. While agreeing with Marx's philosophy of atheism, Darwin rejected his political bias against capitalism.

Theological Complications

In 1831, when the *HMS Beagle* sailed for the four corners of the globe, the discoveries of science and the acceptance of an incredibly well-ordered universe were still largely taken as evidence for the glorious design of an existing Creator God by the British people.

Unfortunately, such belief and trust was gradually displaced by an atmosphere of doubt. This shadowed not only the scientific community, but the church as well. Believers began to face new challenges brought forth by recently proposed theories. For example, Lyell's interpretation of geological evidence had cast increasing suspicion on the Bible's first few chapters, particularly in relation to the Genesis flood. Soon many religious people accepted the idea that the earth might be millions of years old as a rational explanation of its geological history.

In 1860, only one year after Darwin had published *Origin*, a group of Anglican clergymen wrote a book titled *Essays and Review*, a work which marked a milestone in the Anglican perceptions of the Bible.[23] The authors had absorbed the influence of the uniformitarian geologists

Lyell and Hutton, as well as Darwin's biological explanation for the development of life. Both of these views, they believed, demonstrated the scientific inaccuracy of the Genesis account.

Geology, these clergymen argued, revealed that the Bible was not God's absolute word of truth for all times and all places. They also suggested the Bible was based more on human inspiration than divine revelation. *Essays and Reviews* was designed to set the new ideas of science—ideas which opposed the Bible—directly before the British people.

One message came through loud and clear—modern man had progressed far beyond his past ancestors. Understanding the Bible, the authors declared, should incorporate such improvements into current knowledge. Christianity must alter its position and keep in step with the times.

> The Christian religion is in a false position when all the tendencies of knowledge are opposed to it. Such a position can not long be maintained, or can only end in the withdrawal of the educated classes from the influence of religion.[24]

Theological challenges to the Bible began to surface everywhere. Could one believe in Darwin's hypothesis and still hold to the account of creation in Genesis to be true? How should God's action as a creator be perceived in relation to the evolutionary formation of new creatures? Could one continue to use the popular argument for the existence of God, that design requires the existence of a designer?

But the greatest question, the one that struck at the heart of the sacred Scriptures, was even more critical: If human beings evolved from lower animals to a higher state of intellectual and moral consciousness, *how could there be any place for the historic fall of man?*

Armed with what was believed to be irrefutable evidence based upon sound human reasoning and "scientific" fact, a few "leading lights" of the church were soon expressing their own concerns. Some had always had doubts and questions about biblical miracles. Now, in this new Age of Enlightenment, the support of the scientific community encouraged them to express their feelings openly.

Ian Taylor, in his book *In the Minds of Men*, details an event which indicates that some of the most influential church leaders were being skillfully cultivated as apostles of the new faith:

> The first edition of the *Origin* was published in London on 24 November 1859, and contemporary accounts give rise to the oft-repeated statement that an eager public bought up the entire first issue of 1,250 copies on the first day. That the publisher, John Murray sold the entire issue is not in doubt, but the assertion that it was bought by an eager public has been questioned by Freeman,[25] since the book was not even advertised. What seems more probable is that most, if not all, the first issue was bought up by... an agent of Lyell and Hooker [Joseph Hooker, a friend of Darwin's who supported his evolutionary thesis] a week or so before the official date of publication. These copies were then sent gratis to known sympathizers in positions of influence.[26]

One of these sympathizers was amateur naturalist, author, and Anglican clergyman Charles Kingsley. He received a copy of the Darwin's *Origin* and returned a letter of thanks. "Kingsley's letter of thanks to Darwin was dated 18 November 1859; he must have received it a full week before the official publication date. Kingsley wrote, 'I must give up much which I have believed and written.' "[27]

To underscore the victory, Darwin refers to Kingsley's acknowledgement in the second edition of *Origin*:

> A celebrated author and divine has written to me that he has gradually learned to see that it is just as noble a conception of the Deity to believe that He created a few original forms capable of self development into other needful forms, as to believe that He required a fresh act of creation to supply the voids caused by the actions of His laws.[28]

Darwin's Bulldog

Another key player in the struggle between the evolutionary view and the Bible was Thomas Huxley (1825-1895). Huxley was a distinguished biologist and one of Darwin's loudest supporters. For Huxley, Darwinian evolution explained the intricate design of living things. But even more important to Huxley was the fact that evolution allowed him to attack with a vengeance the established clergy whom he so deeply despised.

Thomas Huxley became well known throughout the land as a self-appointed bulldog for the Darwinian cause. Huxley's motivating force was his animosity towards the clergy. Up until this time they held a far greater status than scientists. Indeed Darwin's thesis had given Huxley the opportunity he needed to do public battle with church authority.

The Church Compromise

It would be impossible to trace all of the developments that took place as the church began to accommodate the new ideas from the Age of Enlightenment. However, the general path which unfolded can be understood by following the trend among liberal theologians. These men led the way toward conformity with the idea of evolution.

In their desperate desire to make the Bible seem credible and acceptable to the educated elite, many clergymen embraced the concept that the origin and history of life on planet Earth could be interpreted in evolutionary terms. By allowing long periods of time to exist within biblical chronology, and by emphasizing God's presence in nature and the gradual progression of life toward the emergence of man, they pressed the Bible's account of origins into the evolutionary model.

In his book *The Testimony of the Rocks*, Hugh Miller (1802-1856) interpreted the literal 24-hour days (as described in the Bible) of the creation week as epochs, or extremely long periods of time.[29] This idea later became known as the "day-age" theory, the view that the Bible can easily accommodate a very old earth.

Another theory attempting to integrate the new, revised geological time scale was outlined by an evangelical professor of divinity at Edinburgh, Thomas Chalmers (1780-1847). Chalmers proposed an idea, often called the "gap" theory, in which he suggested millions of years of time could have taken place between Genesis 1:1, and Genesis 1:2.

Chalmers explained that Genesis 1:1, "In the beginning God created the heaven and the earth. And the earth was without form, and void, and darkness was upon the face of the deep," referred to a pre-Adamic race about which the

Scriptures were silent.[30] His central argument was based on the idea that the majority of the fossil record fit well into this period of time.

With these theories designed to attempt to explain the expanded time frame for the history of the earth, theologians then searched for alternatives to the Genesis account of creation. The birth of a new view called "theistic evolution" was a compromise between the biblical and evolutionary worldviews of creation, which called into question the legitimacy of the Bible as a valid historical account of creation.

Spreading Evolution Abroad

Little by little, the concept of theistic evolution began to spread far and wide. In America, one of the most enthusiastic supporters of theistic evolution was Asa Gray (1810-1888), a Harvard professor of botany. Gray used his influence in every way he could to promote Darwin's views.

Gray exerted considerable influence by writing articles and making public presentations. He even tried to persuade Darwin to adopt the position of theistic evolution.[31] Darwin quickly struck down Gray's argument: "The view that each variation has been providentially arranged seems to me to make Natural Selection entirely superfluous, and indeed takes the whole case of the appearance of new species out of the range of science."[32]

Although Gray never went so far to proclaim that the ape was the Adam of Genesis, a professor from Yale University by the name of James Dana (1813-95) did. Dana, who was a Christian, abandoned some of his former beliefs and became a convinced Darwinist after reading *Origin*. He accepted Gray's view of theistic evolution and promoted it wherever he could with great enthusiasm.[33]

Dana almost single-handedly converted Yale from a traditional belief in Christianity to an acceptance of the evolutionary view based on Asa Gray's argument that the evolution of life can be supported from a theistic view. One of Dana's own claims was that he had made Yale a stronghold of evolutionary science, able to "correct false dogma in the theological systems."[34]

Many Christians accepted theistic evolution as a perfect scientific solution. Perhaps, they justified, God *had* used natural processes as His method of creation, and *had* guided evolution to the final realization of man. Perhaps the creation of life as described in Genesis was nothing more than allegory or myth. Perhaps man needed to adopt a flexible point of view which allowed God a wide latitude in His method of creation.

All of the above reasoning, however, only weakens the power of God to be able to rise above man's imagination and his alleged scientific explanations of the origin of life. Theistic evolution is a dangerous device used to annihilate faith and belief in God and His Word.

Evolution and Catholicism

Protestant Christians in England and America were not the only ones to feel the growing repercussions of the acceptance of theistic evolution. Catholics were also deeply affected.

Today it would be safe to say that the vast majority of the people who make up the Catholic church accept an evolutionary explanation for the origin of life. Pope John Paul II has made his own convictions on the subject of theistic evolution very clear. In a statement to a general audience, January 29, 1986, he declared, "Indeed the theory of natural evolution, understood in the sense that it does not exclude divine causality, is not in principle opposed to the truth about creation of the visible world as presented in the Book of Genesis."[35]

Tielhard de Chardin

Of particular note in Catholicism was philosopher, paleontologist, and Jesuit, Pierre Tielhard de Chardin (1881-1955). One of the most widely read Roman Catholic thinkers of his time, de Chardin advanced a new and controversial idea which was based on a combination of theistic evolution and Eastern mysticism. Even though his works were banned for sale in Catholic bookstores by the Vatican in 1957, his influence has touched millions within and without the Catholic church.

According to his esoteric view, human life is part of an interconnectedness with all life and matter. His basic theme is nothing short of pantheism repackaged with new terminology and evolutionary jargon.

Chardin's presumptions of mankind's ascent into higher consciousness may be even more significant today than they were in his own time. His message is identical to the emerging philosophical worldview being embraced by our society. Sadly, even many Charismatic churches are being affected, as we will see later.

Evolution's Legacy

The emergence of evolutionary theory represents the greatest intellectual revolution of the nineteenth century. It changed man's overall perspective of the universe and his place in it. It has since influenced virtually every aspect of science, philosophy, and religion. The sociological implications of the evolutionary theory are immeasurable.

Not only has Darwinian evolution fashioned the way our society perceives this planet's past, it also offers a belief system for those who would, as secular humanists, predict and shape the future of our world, and our children's world. It is time, therefore, to examine evolution's claims, to see whether evolution deserves the position of authority in our culture that it has usurped.

PART 2

The Case for Intelligent Design

CHAPTER 5

The Search for Proof

The first billion, billion, billion, billionth of a second—and then, using a simple system of logic, we can now deduce in exact detail what happened during the first second of creation.... To the astonishment of the lay person, scientists are pushing back the barriers of time to reconstruct the first billion, billion, billion, billionth of a second.[1]

—April Lawton
Science Digest

Everyone recognizes the universe had to have a beginning. It is difficult for the human mind to comprehend what might have taken place when the universe began, yet surprisingly many evolutionist scientists are able to assert with absolute confidence, how, when and where, it all began. They claim that an explosion of an original lump of matter sent material rocketing outward with unbelievable velocity and force and formed the galaxies and solar system.

The "big bang" theory of evolution is built upon the

foundation that all design and complexity observed in the universe can be traced back to this one initial explosion. Scientists suggest this explosion took place between 9 and 18 billion years ago. At that time, scientists claim, all the matter in the universe was packed together in a dense mass at temperatures of many trillions of degrees.

Following the explosion, random chance processes taking place over enormous periods of time were supposedly responsible for the formation of order from disorder. First, atoms and molecules came together to form heavenly bodies like our solar system; billions of years later non-living molecules came together to form simple life; over millions of more years of random processes simple life progressed to form complex life.

From a logical point of view, it is difficult to accept that an explosion was the creative force behind all design and complexity we see in the universe. Especially in light of the obvious fact that all the explosions ever observed have brought about chaotic disorder.

Our common sense tells us no intelligent person would ever attempt to blow up an object with the hope of obtaining another object of greater complexity, no matter how much time was allowed. It is a simple fact—explosions produce disorder out of order. The chance of an explosion being the source of our origins has been noted to surpass the logic of an explosion in a print shop resulting in the formation of an unabridged dictionary.

Not only do logic and common sense make any other outcome seem preposterous, but the laws of physics also contradict the "big bang" hypothesis. Every system allowed to proceed on its own always goes in a direction from order to disorder. This law of the universe is commonly known as the second law of thermodynamics.

A few examples of how this law works will help to illustrate the impossibility of an explosion ever bringing about order from disorder. If you were to take a number of bricks and stack them in a neatly ordered pile, given time, the pile would eventually break down and become disordered. Or if you were to take a brand new car, place it in a garage, and leave it there for 100 years without using it, it would eventually deteriorate, not become something better. All of us can relate to the process of aging. Given time, the cells of our bodies begin to malfunction; we become older, and eventually die.

Both logic and the plain observable evidence contradict the suggestion that an explosion was the creative force behind the beginning of the universe. The only other explanation which seems reasonable is the foundational principle of the creation model: "In the beginning, God."

Testing the Models

It is important to understand that both evolution and creation scientists have accumulated the same data. Both have access to the same information. But the interpretation of the results are biased by the outlook of each scientist. Evolutionary scientists are presenting information as they see it through their philosophical lenses, without respect for the supernatural. Creation scientists are evaluating the same information through the bias of their beliefs based in the Bible, which of course implies supernatural intervention by the Creator of the universe.

While evolution and creation can be *discussed* scientifically, neither can be considered a scientific *theory*, because neither can be "tested" through true scientific experimentation. We cannot go back in time to legitimize, evaluate, or recreate the origin of life. No calculated tests, no trial and error, can confirm or reject the evolutionary concept of origins. And if evolution is still going on, it is impossible to verify or reject it through scientific tests.

Many scientists have commented on this difficulty. Paul Ehrlich and L.C. Birch, two leading biologists, write in their book *Evolutionary History and Population Biology*:

> Our theory of evolution has become...one which cannot be refuted by any possible observations. It is thus "outside of empirical science," but not necessarily false. No one can think of ways in which to test it.... [Evolutionary ideas] have become part of an evolutionary dogma accepted by most of us as part of our training.[2]

Similarly, Peter Medawar, in his book *Mathematical Challenges to the Neo-Darwinism Interpretation of Evolution* states, "It is too difficult to imagine or envisage an evolutionary episode which could not be explained by the formulae of neo-Darwinism."[3] Mr. Medawar's statement implies that as a theory evolution cannot be denied because it embraces everything in order to accommodate it.

"Charles Darwin himself called evolution 'this grand view of life,'" writes Dr. Henry Morris, Ph.D., a creationist scientist. "Evolution is religion, not science....One does not call the law of gravity, for example, 'a satisfactory faith,' nor speak of the laws of thermodynamics as 'dogma.' Evolution is, indeed, 'a grand world view,' but not a science. Its very comprehensiveness makes it impossible even to test scientifically."[4]

Dr. N. Heribert-Nilsson, Director of the Botanical Institute at Lund University, Sweden, has said, "My attempt to demonstrate evolution by an experiment carried on for more than 40 years has completely failed.... The idea of an evolution rests on pure belief."[5]

Finally, one of the world's top evolutionists, Dr. Colin Patterson, senior paleontologist at the British Museum of Natural History, recently called evolution "positively anti-knowledge... all my life I had been duped into taking evolutionism as revealed truth."[6] And on a British Broadcasting telecast he confessed evolution to be "storytelling."

Models, Not Theories

Rather than calling evolution and creation "theories," some creation scientists have suggested a more appropriate alternative term. The Institute for Creation Research, based in California, explains that a better way to think of the evolution/creation debate is in terms of two scientific *models*, an evolution model and a creation model:

> A "model" is a conceptual framework, an orderly system of thought, within which one tries to correlate observable data, and even to predict data. When alternative models exist, they can be compared as to their respective capacities for correlating such data. When, as in this case, neither can be proved, the decision between the two cannot be solely objective. Normally, in such a case, the model which correlates the greater number of data, with the smallest number of unresolved contradictory data, would be accepted as the more probably correct model.... The only way to decide objectively between them, [evolution and creation] therefore, is to note which model fits the facts and predictions with the

smallest number of these secondary assumptions.

Creationists are convinced that, when this procedure is carefully followed, the creation model will always fit the facts as well as or better than the evolution model. Evolutionists may, of course, believe otherwise. In either case, it is important that everyone have the facts at hand with which to consider both models, rather than only one. The latter is brainwashing, not brain-using![7]

From Nonlife to Life

Dr. Robert Jastrow is both a world-famous scientist and a science writer. His career began with training as a physicist at Columbia University. In the late 1950's he joined NASA and set up the Goddard Space Studies in New York. Under his direction, some 200 scientists played key roles in space flights to Jupiter, Saturn, Mercury, and Venus. Jastrow has also received the NASA Medal for Exceptional Scientific Achievement. In *Geo* magazine, February 1982, Dr. Jastrow was asked to explain how nonlife became life:

Basic building blocks of life—amino acids and nucleotides—were made in earth's atmosphere by the passage of lightening bolts through primitive gases. Then they drained out of the atmosphere into the oceans and made a kind of "chicken soup" in which collisions occurred. Eventually, the first self-replicating molecule was formed by accident, and as soon as a molecule could divide and reproduce itself, you had a magic law broken for the first time.

The scientific story of genesis has chance as its basic ingredient. You look at the story in detail, and every element of it is governed by some random event. A random collision among atoms that created stars including the sun. Random collisions of the molecules of life that created the first DNA, the first self-replicating molecule. This fact has both puzzled and distressed many students of the subject. They feel that since the story leads in an unbroken line from that chance event of a threshold straight up to man, there's something unsatisfactory about it, about a story that says man's existence on earth is a product of chance.[8]

Hostile Opposition

Those who do not wholeheartedly agree with this so-called "scientific" explanation for the origin of life are described by Dr. Jastrow as "puzzled" and "distressed." Many evolutionist scientists go much further in claiming that people who question the validity of the theory of evolution by pointing out weaknesses and inconsistencies in it are guilty of pushing science back into the dark ages and "threatening the scientific literacy" of the general public.[9] Those who challenge statements which have been based upon unverifiable assumption and outright speculation are classified as "pea-brained,"[10] "dangerous,"[11] "book-burning censors"[12] who are attempting to "mislead,"[13] and "dupe"[14] society.

Those who would ask the public school system to consider presenting an alternate model for origins (called a "crack-pot theory"[15]) alongside evolution are "abusing science,"[16] "muddying the clear waters of evolution,"[17] and making "responsible teachers deceive their students."[18]

"Inspired Guesses"

Isaac Asimov, science writer, renowned atheist, and president of the American Humanist Association, is not quite as adamant as Robert Jastrow about the initial details of the nonlife to life scenario. He does agree, however, that it did not come about with the aid of a Creator God. He states:

> We can make *inspired guesses*, but we don't know for certain what physical and chemical properties of the planet's crust, its ocean and its atmosphere made it so conducive to such a sudden appearance of life.... Thus the problem that scientists face is how to explain the suddenness with which life appeared on this young [4.6 billion-year-old] planet earth. This is a question that has plagued us ever since the nineteenth century, when scientists first began to accept the concept of biological evolution and to dismiss the possibility that life had been created in its present complexity by some supernatural agency. That raised the question of how this extraordinary phenomenon called life could possibly have come to be by accident (emphasis added).[19]

Asimov dismisses the possibility that life could have been brought into existence by a supernatural creative being. Instead of a Creator, he suggests the best alternative is nothing more than an "inspired guess." It may come as a shock that well-trained and competent scientists who make statements based on fact and measurement would stake their credibility on an "inspired guess."

Spontaneous Generation

The question needs to be asked. *Can* life arise spontaneously from nonlife? Several hundred years ago, it was commonly believed that living things could be produced from nonliving things by the process of spontaneous generation. People believed that if garbage were left outdoors over a period of time, it would eventually turn into maggots, flies, and rats.

A man by the name of Francesco Redi decided he would prove to the world scientifically that living things cannot be produced from nonliving material. He performed a famous experiment in which he placed decaying meat in a group of wide-mouthed jars. Some were covered with lids, some were covered with a fine veil and some were left open. He proved conclusively that maggots only arose where flies were able to lay their eggs.[20] By doing this experiment, Redi showed his generation that living things cannot be produced from nonliving material by the process of spontaneous generation.

The idea that people of the past actually believed in spontaneous generation seems unbelievable to us today. Scientists of the twentieth century would laugh at the simple experiment Redi used to convince intellectuals of his day that they were wrong. And yet the theory of evolution stands on a foundational principle very much like the idea of the spontaneous generation of life that was accepted as scientifically valid in the past. Evolutionary theory accepts without question that nonlife can become life (simple and gradually more complex life) by a process taking place over millions of years of time guided by nothing more than random chance events.

What does observable evidence and logic tell us? The observations made when we examine living things is that all life originates from life which already exists—life comes from preexisting life. This is commonly known in the field of biology as the "law of biogenesis."[21]

The cell is described by biologists as the basic unit of life. No scientist has ever observed a cell originating from nonliving raw materials by spontaneous processes. Even controlled experimentation by the advanced technology of our day has never been able to produce a living cell. Cells can only come from cells that are already in existence.

Multicellular organisms never arise spontaneously from nonliving material. The perpetuation of life can only take place as living things beget a new generation of living things. Plants produce seed which produce new plants of the same kind; cats produce kittens which develop into mature cats. Life can only originate from life which already exists. This is powerful evidence that clearly supports the law of biogenesis and clearly contradicts the evolutionary view.

Complexities of Life

Biology is the field of science dealing with the study of living things. Biologists agree that the more they study the complex structures and systems that make up living things, the more astonishing becomes their view of the complexity of life. In an attempt for us to catch a glimpse of this complexity, let's examine the structure of the cell more closely. All living organisms are composed of cells. The human body, for example, is made up of over 100 *trillion* single cells. Some of these cells are so small that a million of them could occupy a space no larger than a pinhead.

It would be fair to say that a single cell is the most complex structure known to man. It is even more complicated than a human being, since an entire human being originates from one. Every one of us began from a single cell formed as a result of the union of a sperm cell and an egg cell from our parents, which fused together at the time of fertilization. The blueprint for the construction of our entire makeup was contained within the chromosomes in the nucleus of that first cell.

The cell is a micro-universe containing trillions of molecules. These molecules are the structural building blocks for countless complex structures performing chains of complex biochemical reactions with exquisite precision. One biologist has made the following statement regarding the complexity of a cell: "Even if we knew all there is to know about how a cell works, we would still be baffled. How nerve cells create emotions, thoughts, behavior, memory and other perceptions cannot yet, if indeed ever, be described in the language of molecular biology."[22]

Most of us have seen simplified diagrammatic representations of cells depicting various cellular components and their functions. A single cell surrounded by a cellular membrane exhibits the same degree of complexity as a city with all of its systems of operation, communication, and government. There are power plants that generate the cell's energy, factories that produce enzymes and hormones essential for life, complex transportation systems that guide specific chemicals from one location to another, membrane proteins that act as barricades controlling the import and export of materials across the cellular membrane.

Every minute structure within a cell has a specific purpose. Without the full complement of all these structures, the cell cannot function. In fact, even the slightest malfunction within the cell can bring about the immediate termination of its existence. How unbelievable it seems that such awesome complexity could have arisen by chance.

The nucleus is the area within the cell that contains the chromosomes which are made up of DNA molecules that are responsible for the perpetuation of life as it is passed down from one generation to the next. The late Luther Sunderland, author of *Darwin's Enigma*, explains the complexity of the remarkable DNA code. He notes that it is "a twisted little ladderlike molecule which makes up all of our genes and chromosomes":

> As a little pocket calculator has within it a memory which tells it how to operate and do complex calculations, so in the nucleus of every cell is a little computer program that tells the cell how to be part of an organism and do complex functions. The simplest, single-celled organism we know anything about has in its genes and chromosomes about as much data as there are letters in the world's largest library. A ten with twelve zeroes—a trillion letters.[23]

Every one of us started out from a tiny cell no larger than the period at the end of this sentence. All of the coded information required for the development of our entire bodies originated from the DNA of that first cell.

The DNA molecule is so minute and compact, it is hard for our human minds to comprehend. Perhaps the following illustration will help to give us a better understanding. The number of human beings living on the earth has been estimated to be somewhere between 4.5 and 5 billion people. If it were possible to reduce every individual to the original blueprint from which he originated, a container the size of an aspirin tablet could store the blueprints for the entire world's population.[24]

Once again, we are staggered when we consider the awesome complexity of life. It becomes absurd when we consider that evolution accepts that the origin and complexity of life came about by random, accidental processes. Such a claim is a contradiction to sound logical thinking.

Not a Chance!

A final argument for the purposeful design of an intelligent Creator is drawn from the field of bionics. Bionics is a specialized arm of biological engineering, which specifically attempts to mimic processes found in nature. Some of the most amazing inventions man has ever made have come about by the careful study of mechanisms which are in operation in nature. Often when these inventions are referred to, the phrase "bionic comparison" is used. Let's look at some examples of bionic comparisons.

For years men who studied bats tried to find out how these creatures could find their way in the dark. It was eventually discovered that bats navigate by transmitting sound vibrations. The bat sends out high-pitched ultrasonic signals from its vocal organs that bounce off anything in its path. The bat then perceives the signal bounced back to it, and the bat's brain is able to make the necessary response in its flight pattern and to determine what the object is. This is a truly amazing system of design that many scientists claim the process of evolution has developed over millions of years of time.

Man-made radar and sonar systems were designed by studying the bat's system. These highly advanced technological inventions transmit frequencies and measure the time required for these frequencies to be bounced back to the transmitting device. Radar has been heralded as one of man's great accomplishments.

The human eye is another remarkable system. As you are reading this page, light is reflected from the page to your eyes. The light then passes through an opening in the eye called the pupil. The size of the opening, and thus the amount of light allowed to pass through the pupil, is controlled by muscles in the iris. The iris closes down in bright light and opens up when the light becomes dim. The light then passes through a lens. Muscles within the eye control the shape of the lens, focusing the image that you are viewing onto a light-sensitive screenlike retina at the back of the eyeball. Cells in the retina convert the light energy into an electrical stimulus which is then transferred to the brain. The brain then records the information the eye has perceived, and it is stored there for as long as you live.

A video system, engineered by the design of man, functions in very much the same way as the eye. Light reflected by objects is controlled by a mechanical iris and focused by a lens within the video camera. The light energy is converted to an electrical signal, then transmitted to a video recorder where the information is stored for playback at a later time. No one would ever suggest that a video system is the product of random processes of chance over millions of years of time. Yet the eye, which is far more complex, is commonly attributed to the process of evolution—even though Charles Darwin himself said, "To suppose that the eye with all its inimitable contrivances for adjusting the focus to different distances, for admitting different amounts of light, and for the correction of spherical and chromatic aberration, could have been formed by natural selection, seems, I freely confess, absurd in the highest degree."[25]

Often evolutionists will argue that it takes a series of mutations or mistakes in the genetic code to develop higher orders of complexity. Given long periods of time and random chance events major changes can supposedly occur in an organism. But no one has ever been able to explain how this "hit and miss" process could create complex organs like lungs, hearts, or kidneys. How would the immune system come into existence gradually over millions of years of time? It is obvious that creatures with such highly specialized structures essential for survival could not manage to exist while these structures and functions were evolving.

By looking at these examples of bionic comparisons, we can see a pattern of logic. There is no question in our minds that inventions made by man are the result of intelligent design and planning. There is a zero possibility that they could have arisen by spontaneous chance. The same holds true for man himself.

Design Without a Designer

Our society seems compelled to compete in the "fashion" marketplace today. One need only to glance at any smart dresser or at a gathering of style-conscious yuppies to observe that millions of people worldwide are obsessed with the designer clothes they flaunt. Designer labels are conspicuously brandished on apparel to impress all who follow the cult of prestigious clothing.

Yet ironically the same application is not followed with the design of creation. Nature, animals, and man have all the complex attributes of a Designer God behind them, yet

His praise is not flaunted. Instead His label is ripped off and credit is given to a charlatan.

Dr. John Morris clarifies the intuitive argument in his article, "Did a Watchmaker Make the Watch?":

> In the early 1880's, William Paley published a carefully argued paper entitled "Natural Theology," which developed a convincing case for the necessity of a Designer to produce the intricate design we see in living systems.
>
> He referred to human machines such as a watch, claiming we would never conclude, upon discovery of a watch, that it was the result of natural processes such as wind and rain. By observing the order of the organism, the purpose of each part, and the interdependence of the parts, one would never conclude that it happened by chance.
>
> To propose that a living, replicating cell arose without design from non-living matter is easily the weakest point of evolution theory—so weak that many famous scientists who have worked for years to find a plausible way it might have happened have concluded that life evolved somewhere out in space where conditions are different from those here on Earth, because it evidently could not happen here.[26]

Although unwilling to grant the credit of creation to the power of an unlimited Designer, Dr. Francis Crick, a Nobel Prize-winning geneticist, acknowledges that "an honest man, armed with all the knowledge available to us now, could only state that in some sense, the origin of life appears at the moment to be almost a miracle, so many are the conditions which would have had to have been satisfied to get it going."[27]

Dr. Lewis Thomas, M.D., in writing the forward for a National Geographic publication called *The Incredible Machine*, claims the title of the book is appropriate. The word "machine" comes from the ancient Indo-European word "magh" meaning "power" from which we derive the closely related word "magic." His concluding statement sums up many an evolutionist's view of why we are here: "Incredible magic, that's what we are, and that's what this book is all about."[28]

Incredible magic or intelligent design? The arguments of reason all point to intelligent design. There remains, however, a second building block of evolutionary theory that must be examined and refuted. If creation *has* occurred, and evolution *has not*, what are we to make of the evolutionists' so-called "missing links"? Do they not prove evolution's claims? (For further reading see *The Evidence for Creation* by McLean and Oakland and the Recommended Reading list.)

CHAPTER 6

Missing Links

The "missing links" that troubled Darwin and his followers are no longer missing.[1]

—National Academy
of Sciences
Science and Creationism

It's completely false to say that there's a lacking of transitional forms. We have plenty of them—more than sometimes we can cope with.[2]

—Dr. Louis S. Russel,
Director, Royal Ontario Museum

Evolutionists agree that after the first major quantum leap from nonlife to the first cell the progression from molecule to man was well on its way. Single-celled organisms, over millions of years, randomly developed into multicellular plants and animals. Animals without backbones, over millions of years, developed into fish. Fish, over more millions of years and chance events, crawled out from the water onto the land, sprouted legs and became amphibians. Then amphibians gradually developed into reptiles. Reptiles with scales developed wings and became birds with feathers or became fur-bearing mammals. Finally, after countless more millions of years of time, mammals eventually walked upright and developed into apes, and eventually into the human kind. And here we are!

Who would have the audacity to question such a scientific explanation for this "magical" journey from molecule to man?

Perhaps the greatest ally to the entire evolution view is the simple factor of extremely long periods of time. It allows the evolutionist the freedom to choose such words as "developed," "gradually changed," and "eventually progressed." Relegating mystical events to a period of history in the far-distant past has always been an effective way to make fantasy more realistic. "It happened a long, long, long time ago" begin the authors of untold numbers of fairy tales. A princess kisses a frog and it becomes a prince—that's called a fairy tale. Millions of years ago a frog became a man—and that's called science!

Before biological evolution could be proposed, it was necessary to lay the foundation that the earth was billions of years old and that layers of the earth had been laid down gradually over millions and millions of years of time. As we saw earlier, James Hutton and Charles Lyell were responsible for providing this concept, and their objective was to come up with an alternative view to creationism.

How do long periods of time act as a magic factor to make things that don't seem possible appear reasonable? Suppose someone walked into a university biology department and proposed a brand-new theory for the origin of mankind. They claimed that a single-celled organism such as an amoeba could become a man, given a few minutes of time. Obviously such an idea would be termed ridiculous and rejected as nothing more than fantasy.

But long periods of time change this proposition drastically. If the same individual went to the same university with the same idea, claiming an amoeba could become a man, but that it would take millions of years of time and chance, his view would be welcomed with open arms. And of course that is exactly what has happened with the Darwinian tree of life which pictures a single-celled amoeba at the bottom and a man at the top. Long periods of time have made a ridiculous idea seem credible.

The Progression of Life

If evolution is true, there should be countless transitional forms showing the progression of life from one kind to another. If random and undirected evolution occurred permitting free development in many different directions, then there should be obvious examples showing how this has taken place. The fossils embedded in the crust of the earth should show the record of the transition of life-forms in the past. We should be able to identify living things in the process of change from one kind to another.

Evolutionary science claims that we have such evidence. Two well-respected researchers who were interviewed on-camera for the film *The Evolution Conspiracy* firmly stated their belief that this was so:

There are myriad transitional forms. There's really no problem finding them—*Dr. Leo Hickey*, Former Director, Yale Peabody Museum.

In fact, there are so many transitional forms between species that we must often fall back on statistical analysis to separate one from another—*Dr. Preston Cloud*, Director of Geological Science, University of California (Santa Barbara).

But when pressed during the course of the interviews, both scientists admitted their dilemma:

> One of the things that also make it a little more difficult in the fossil record is the rapidity with which evolution acts in very short bursts. It doesn't leave many transitional forms behind— *Dr. Hickey.*

> The problem of transitional forms is one that all honest paleontologists have a problem with. The geological record is incomplete. It's incomplete because of erosion—*Dr. Cloud.*

Clues to the Past

Fossils are the record or the remains of plants and animals living in the past found preserved in the earth's crust, and are the primary evidence used as historical documentation of earlier life. The process of fossilization is seen to be a mystery unable to be duplicated to explain the massive global preservation of life of the past. It is the result of mineralization in conditions that turn the organic materials (bones, leaves, etc.) to rock in a short period of time. Fossils are the verdict of a giant graveyard and, creationists believe, the conclusion of a devastating world upheaval, described in the Bible as Noah's flood.

Evolutionists do admit that catastrophic deposition produces fossils, but explain that today's fossil evidence was caused by many local floods depositing material over millions of years. However, local floods cannot adequately explain the evidence of massive "bone beds." "Bone beds" are enormous deposits of devastation with millions of crushed and fossilized bones of hundreds of dinosaurs. Asking evolutionists how these deposits could have been the result of local floods and gradual deposition produces very weak answers.

Today, fossils worldwide show that thousands of different kinds of animals lived together during the same time period, and that through some incredibly powerful disaster were thrown from ocean beds into the middle of land masses and up mountains, and preserved in the depths of the earth. Extensive searches throughout the world have not uncovered any evidence that one type of animal ever changed into another type of animal, that frogs came from fishes, that reptiles changed to birds or that man descended from apelike creatures.

No "intermediary fossils," that is, "fossils in the middle stages" of development between fish and bird, or mammal and man, have ever been discovered to prove that such a theory is more than merely speculation. Charles Darwin himself said that the fossil record was "perhaps the most obvious and serious objection" to his theory.

Missing Links Still Missing

In an attempt to explain away the lack of evidence of transitional forms in the fossil record many evolutionists claim that evolution takes place over millions of years and is too slow to be observable. Another, more recent, explanation says that it is happening too fast for us to see.

This newest modification is called punctuated equilibria, and it is yet another theory resulting from lack of evidence to support the original theory! Such circular reasoning is certainly a challenge to logic.

Punctuated equilibria supposes that a group of species

breaks away from the parent group of species and rapidly develops into a new species. With this model of biology paleontologists are now able to explain away the lack of fossil evidence.

Still, the fact remains that there is no evidence in the fossil record to support either gradual or rapid evolution. Under normal reasoning one would deduce such a lack of evidence to be a positive conclusion that no species have ever changed into another, as the evolution hypothesis maintains. Rather, the opposite has occurred. The evidence that hasn't been found in nearly a hundred and fifty years of diligent searching is called "the missing link," and hundreds of scientists continue in their attempts to find evidence that missing links are indeed missing. Sound scientific reasoning!

The concept of evolution is a hypothetical assumption. It should not be confused with science, which *Webster's Dictionary* defines as "knowledge derived from observation, facts and principles."

When animals die they are not normally fossilized. Their carcasses usually decompose and rot, or perhaps scavengers eat their remains. If left unprotected, the elements may destroy much of the personal information regarding the creature.

Even so, many scientists have convinced the public that the fossil record is replete with examples of missing links. Most often these missing links are confirmed not by factual evidence but rather by the use of hypothetical artistic representations. Science textbooks are full of proposals and illustrations supposedly proving the existence of transitional forms. Museums often display models of fishlike creatures crawling out on the land, then growing legs instead of fins, and so on. But what are these models based on?

Many evolutionists attempt to determine characteristics like hair color, skin tones, and features that are not possible to deduce from fossil finds. Bent on fitting the evidence into their evolutionary worldview, they conjecture how many millions of years old the evidence is, what animal it was before it came to be found in its present state, what it ate while in another state, or how it walked before it became what the fossil evidence states it to be at the time of the finding. The same is true of fossilized bones. Bones, if not smashed beyond recognition, may certainly be identified without too much trouble as belonging to a dog or a cow. But the color of the skin or hair of that dog or cow may not be deduced from the bone! These attempts, at best, are wild imaginary guesses, and at worst, the propagation of a theory based around the bias of the person who found the fossil or bone. The conclusion cannot be supposed to be a sound scientific evaluation, but a furthering of a philosophy of life.

Dr. Colin Patterson of the British Museum of Natural History is refreshingly straightforward about the lack of evidence for transitional forms. When questioned by Dr. Luther Sunderland about the lack of such forms in his book on fossils, *Evolution*, Dr. Patterson, who has millions of fossils in his museum collection, wrote, "I fully agree with your comments on the lack of direct illustrations of transitional forms in my book. If I knew of any, fossil or living creature, I would certainly have included them." Later he added, "I will lay it on the line, there is not one such fossil for which one might make a watertight argument."[3]

Yet millions of people are being sold a bill of evolutionary goods!

A Whale of a Tale

The whale is often used by scientists as an example of evolution. Theory suggests that primitive mammalian ancestors lived on land before developing into marine-dwelling creatures. It is proposed that the whale's ancestor had legs which later evolved into flippers. Over the past several years, evolutionists have made serious attempts to locate a fossil that would substantiate this theory.

Science Digest, November 1980, contains an article titled, "Whales With Legs." The reader is shown an artist's illustration of a whalelike creature with legs and told the following:

> Not far from the Khyber Pass in the arid Himalayan foothills of Pakistan, University of Michigan paleontologist, Phillip Gingerich, found a skull and several teeth, and came to the startling conclusion that they had belonged to an ancient walking whale. Gingerich is returning to the Himalayan foothills this fall to find more fossils so he can piece together a clearer picture of the whale's evolutionary history...he hopes to find leg bones belonging to the whale species. "It is possible that we will find some," he says, "but we will be lucky if we do."[4]

It is apparent that artists' conceptions without all of the facts can be very misleading, and millions of people accept such conjecture as fact. Speculation cannot be classified as science, and is certainly not adequate information to show a transitional life-form.

Archeopteryx: Spreading Its Evolutionary Wings

Another popular example of a proposed missing link is a fossil named Archeopteryx. This creature is claimed by most evolutionists to be the link that ties together the bird family with reptiles.[5] The fossil indicates that this creature had feathers, wings, and a beak. Other characteristics Archeopteryx exhibits that have led paleontologists to seek a tie with the reptiles are the presence of teeth in its mouth and claws on its wings.

These two characteristics do not prove Archeopteryx evolved from reptiles. Birds like the ostrich have claws on their wings and they are obviously classified as birds. Although there are no living birds with teeth in their mouths, there are many examples of birds in the fossil record that have teeth. Some reptiles have teeth, and some do not, so this characteristic should not be particularly important in distinguishing birds from reptiles.

Science News, in its September 24, 1977 issue, mentions a bird fossil that was found in Colorado. Dating of this particular specimen by radiometric techniques gave an age of over 140 million years. This is as old or older than the proposed age for Archeopteryx. If Archeopteryx can be classified as a link between reptiles and birds as evolutionists claim, then the age for fossils of birds would have to be younger. However this is not the case. By evolutionists' own measure of radiometric dating the impossibility of making the Archeopteryx an ancestor of birds is confirmed.

But stop for a moment and think of some of the incredible changes that would be required for the evolution of birds from reptiles. Scales would have to become feathers.

Front legs would have to become wings. The skeletal system would have to be lightened. The body metabolism would have to change drastically in order to provide enough energy for flight. It seems rather impossible that all of these major changes could suddenly happen by chance. And even if they did, where is the evidence of intermediate forms?

The process of learning to fly also poses questions which cannot be resolved by the fossil record. Numerous suggestions put forward by scientists outline the evolution of flight in birds. *Science Yearbook* explains: "Most paleontologists assumed that Archeopteryx could fly, or at least glide from tree to tree. They assumed that the bird's ancestors learned to climb trees to escape from predators and to seek insect food. Once the bird was in the tree, feathers and wings evolved to aid in gliding from branch to branch."[6]

Paleontologist John H. Ostrum of Yale University in New Haven, Connecticut, presents a different view. He believes that Archeopteryx learned to fly from the ground up, and not from the trees down. He states, "Carnivores ran along the ground chasing flying insects, which they nabbed with their teeth or their front legs. Longer feathers on the front legs evolved to act as an insect net, and so the legs became wings. Then they used the wings to make flapping leaps after insects."[7]

It is obvious these two "scientific" suggestions for the origin of bird flight are nothing more than pure speculation and perhaps humorous imagination. Certainly not all evolutionary scientists make such wild speculations. And in no way do we want to leave the impression that all evolutionists are intentionally deceiving the public. But the fact remains, there are those who are driven by a desire to come up with something new and spectacular. After all, revolutionary discoveries make headlines.

Luther Sunderland, in his book *Darwin's Enigma*, described an interview he held with Dr. Niles Eldridge, a curator at the Museum of Natural History in New York. Eldridge was asked what he thought about piecing together evolutionary scenarios. He stated: "Such accounts are limited only by one's own imagination and the credulity of the audience.... As science, it doesn't wash."[8]

Crossopterygian: Finding the Fountain of Youth

For years the Crossopterygian, a fish, was maintained by evolutionists to have certain limblike characteristics supposedly indicating that it was advancing from the fish to the amphibian stage. Evolutionists claimed this creature had become extinct approximately 90 million years ago. Because of this assumption, the Crossopterygian was often used as an index fossil for dating layers of the earth. Whenever a Crossopterygian fossil was found it was immediately determined that the layer it was found in had to be at least 90 million years old.

However, in 1939 a living relative of the Crossopterygian, the Coelocanth, was caught off the coast of Madagascar, near Africa.[9] Since then many of these creatures have been observed. Obviously the Coelocanth can no longer be used as an index fossil to date the layers of the earth. No longer can it be cited as an example of a fossil that shows the evolution of life from one kind to another.

Simple Horse Sense

Nearly every natural history museum has a chart or series of fossils or models showing the documented evolution of the modern-day, single-toed horse from a smallish, four-toed creature over millions of years of time. What is often overlooked is the fact that the series is assembled from fossils found in India, South America, North America, and Europe, which have been arranged in a neat sequential order of size from the smallest to the largest. The reality is that nowhere in the world are the fossils of the horse series found in successive strata.

In addition, when the rib pairs of the members in the chart are compared we see a startling discrepancy. The four-toed member has 18 pairs, the next creature has 19, then there is a drop to 15, and finally back to 18 pairs for the modern horse. Certainly, there is a great deal of speculation involved in the formation of such a chart. And there is no proof whatsoever that one member of the chart ever evolved into another.

The four-toed "horse" called Eohippus does not look the least bit like a true horse. When it was first found it was classified as a rabbitlike creature. Interestingly, fossils of this oldest member of the alleged evolutionary horse chart have been found in the surface strata along with modern horses.[10]

Today, numbers of scientists who are committed evolutionists do not accept the scientific validity of the chart depicting the evolution of the horse. In spite of this, the chart continues to be used in science books as factual proof for the theory of evolution.

Monkey Business

Since Darwin's idea of descent from a common ancestor became well known in the late 1800's, many individuals have been consumed by a burning desire to climb down the branches of the human family tree and examine its roots.

As the following statement reflects, for some the evidence leaves little room for doubt about our genealogy:

> Studies in evolutionary biology have led to the conclusion that mankind arose from ancestral primates. This association was hotly debated among scientists before Darwin's day, before molecular biology and the discovery of the now abundant connecting links. Today, however, there is no significant scientific doubt about the close evolutionary relationships among all primates or between apes and humans.[11]

Evolutionists start with the assumption man has evolved from the ape, then attempt to assemble the evidence in order to support their case. The picture portrayed is that apes swung out of the jungle, lost their tales, and started their journey on the road to higher consciousness.

But not always do the bold and confident conclusions drawn by evolutionary scientists line up with the facts. As we've seen with "lower" animals, the closest we can come to encountering our so-called early human ancestors is through paintings and sculptures created by artists who work with anthropologists. Unfortunately, fossil fragments and bits of jaw bones and teeth say nothing about the fleshy parts of nose, lips and ears. Hairiness is a matter of pure conjecture. But the evolutionary mindset is consumed by the idea that the older the specimen is said to be, the more primitive it must look. Once again, critical thinking is essential when we are given the opportunity to examine the proposed evolution from ape to man.

Over the past several decades evolutionists have proposed a small number of links in the lineage of man. However, upon close examination many have proven to be based on either inadequate or outright fraudulent evidence. A good example to begin with is Nebraska Man.

Nebraska Man

In 1922, a single molar tooth was found in a layer of earth in Nebraska. Professor Henry Osborn, head of the American Museum of Natural History, described it as belonging to an early ape-man. He named it "Hesperopithecus harold cooki," honoring its founder, a geologist by the name of Harold Cook.[12]

In June of 1922, the *Illustrated London News* published an artist's conception of the Nebraska Man as well as his mate. The tooth was all the evidence there was, so the artist was instructed to depict something part-ape and part-man.[13]

The magazine had worldwide distribution, and it was not long before Nebraska Man was heralded as evidence for a "missing link." In fact, when the famous Scopes Trial took place in Dayton, Ohio, in July 1925, Nebraska Man was firmly established as one of the absolute proofs of evolution. Shortly after the trial, in 1928, it was discovered that a mistake had been made and the tooth from which Nebraska Man had been constructed was the tooth of an extinct pig.[14]

"Lucy"—The Woman Who Shook Man's Family Tree

In the mid-1970's, in the Afar triangle of Ethiopia, noted paleontologist Carl Johanson and his party discovered the now-famous and controversial "Lucy" skeleton, which Dr. Johanson has claimed "comes closer to representing what the average person thinks of as the missing link than any other fossil found in Africa."[15] Lucy was supposed to be one of the first creatures in the lineage of ape to man to have walked upright and, as Johanson states, "has extraordinary importance in terms of understanding the very early stages of human evolution."[16] Johanson goes on:

> As you know, Lucy was found in 1974. I sometimes refer to her as the woman who shook up man's family tree because she represents for us the oldest, most complete skeleton we have of any human ancestor known to anthropologists.[17]

Despite Dr. Johanson's description of the "most complete skeleton," it is interesting to note that his find was less than 40 percent complete. Fragments of fossilized bones included parts of the skull, rib cage, arms, pelvis, leg bones, and a single knee joint. He described his find enthusiastically:

> I happened to glance over my right shoulder into an area that we had not surveyed, an area that we had missed that morning. And there on the surface was a little bit of elbow and I recognized it immediately as belonging to a human ancestor. I knew it wasn't a monkey or a gazelle or anything else. We gave it a terrible tongue twister of a name called "australopithecus afarensis" or the ape-person of the Afar region in Ethiopia.[18]

Such a tremendous discovery is something that most paleoanthropologists only dream of. Johanson described his excitement in a *National Geographic* article this way:

> "We found it, we found it," I shouted.... A hominid skeleton just lying there waiting to be

collected.... Surely such a noble little fossil lady deserved a name. As we sat around one evening listening to the Beatles' songs, someone said, "Why don't we call her Lucy? You know, after 'Lucy in the Sky with Diamonds.'" So she became Lucy.[19]

In *Time* magazine January 29, 1979, Johanson described his find as "an exciting and provocative breakthrough." The article, titled "The Lucy Link," mentions that *"even before Johanson assembled* Lucy's remaining bones, he could see that she had been bipedal [able to walk upright]: the clue was a telling knee joint" (emphasis ours).

More than 12 years later, at a gathering of over 800 people at the University of Missouri, Johanson was confronted on the issue of the "telling knee joint." Johanson claimed that it was more humanlike than chimplike. In a question and answer period following the presentation, a creationist pressed Johanson for more specific information on the location where the knee joint was found. "How far away from Lucy did you find the knee?" he asked. Johanson answered reluctantly, "In a strata 200 feet lower and over a mile and a half away."[20]

Johanson's statement to *Time* magazine that *even before he assembled* Lucy's bones he could see that she had been bipedal displays overtones of irresponsible conspiracy in the battle to advance evolutionism.

In a February 1981 issue of *Newsweek*, reporters Peter Gwynne and John Caley highlight a number of disputes surrounding controversial paleoanthropologists from Charles Darwin to modern scientists. They cite "soap opera details of personal prejudices, bitter rivalries and twists of fortune that frequently make science as Machiavellian as politics."[21] The article continues with the admission that "scanty [fossil] evidence, often incorrectly understood," is all that exists. "You could put all of the fossils on the top of a single desk," said Elwyn Simons of Duke University.

And a *Time* article reports, "Scientists concede that even their most cherished theories are based on embarrassingly few fossil fragments, and that huge gaps exist in the fossil record."[22]

Back to the Creation Model

If our attempts to trace the lineage from molecule to man has produced nothing more than an embarrassing puzzle, is there not some other reasonable alternative?

Scientists' only tool to discover the past is through the evidence of today's existing fossil record. A scientist doesn't know everything because he doesn't have the evidence before him to know everything. However, God has imparted all the wisdom and knowledge needed to come to the right conclusions in the Bible. All evidence found to date qualifies the Bible as true and reliable. After a century and a half of futile attempts to prove Darwin's radical assertions, it's time to give the Bible another look.

A jigsaw puzzle provides a simple analogy. The box containing the pieces has a helpful picture of the completed puzzle on its front. If the pieces don't fit the overall picture, one would have to assume that the wrong bits are in the box. So far all evidence found in the fossil record has supported the theory of creation. Much to the evolutionists' chagrin, they have had to continually change and modify their theories to fit new findings.

Most of the fossils found today, whether molds or casts or petrified specimens, are probably the result of an enormous, powerful flood—one of global proportions—which the Bible refers to in Genesis. Noah, his family, and the animals which God deemed necessary were preserved in an ark made to God's specifications and design (Genesis 6:19,20; 7:2,3).

Highly incredible? Fossil evidence supports the biblical account, yet not only do humanist scientists and evolutionists disregard the facts, but ashamedly many prominent Christian pastors, teachers, and leaders do too.

These leaders have lost the very essence and foundation of Christianity—faith in the authority of the Bible and the One who inspired it. Such a lack of faith in the absolute integrity of God's Word leads not only to the destruction of believers' faith, but also their hope.

Fossils do not prove evolution or creation; however, they do support the biblical account of the origin of life which states that God created animals and fish, birds and man, each according to its own kind, from the very beginning of His creation of life.

Evolution excludes the power and authority of the Judeo-Christian God and discredits the authenticity of the Judeo-Christian Bible. Yet it is a religion in its own right because it pursues wisdom of ultimate reality. Demanding much faith, and built around a specific system of beliefs, evolution manufactures a philosophy of life which spiritualizes that cosmic forces and natural powers birthed life and nature. Evolution stands in stark contrast to the model of creation.

CHAPTER 7

God's Grand Design

I f evolution wasn't God's design, what was? The creation model is built squarely on the foundation of the Christian's faith in the Word of God, the Bible. And the Bible begins with the book of Genesis.

The first 11 chapters of Genesis teach that God created man as man. Jesus—and all nine New Testament authors after Him—quoted liberally from the first 11 chapters of Genesis. Creation was the worldview of the people to whom Jesus spoke. The Psalms, Proverbs, Isaiah, Jeremiah, Job, and Genesis all speak of the Lord as the Maker of the world, and Jesus also quoted extensively from those writings. More important, in Mark 10:6 He verified that God created man and woman "from the beginning of the creation."

Moses taught that God made the world, and that the zenith of His creation was Adam and Eve. Genesis 1 and 2 tell of a creation that took God six literal days. It says that God marked off each day with a beginning and an end, "And the evening and the morning were the first day..." and so forth. He supernaturally made bewildering elements, lavish plants, extraordinary fish, colorful birds, varieties of animals, and ultimately man.

After forming man with personal tender care from the dust of the earth, God put His mouth to him, "and breathed into his nostrils the breath of life." Man was created intentionally in the image of God, "...after our likeness." This uniqueness was given to man alone and not other lifeforms. It is what makes up his moral nature. His body, spirit, and soul form a tri-unity, and in it there is a part that has consciousness of God. This privilege of man soars above the life given to the rest of God's creation.

With life (spirit, soul and body) God gave man a free will and the choice of doing either good or evil. God explained that with doing good would come blessing but warned that to indulge in evil would bring the consequence of death—a hitherto unknown commodity.

Man defied God's edict with a willful act of disobedience. God was true to His word, and death entered into God's creation. Man's decision to take the law into his own hands subjected him to several consequences that have affected every generation since. Outside the Garden man became more and more defiled. Sin diminished his desire to be in fellowship with his Creator. He deviated from God's morality, becoming stubborn, contrary, and disobedient. Genesis 6:5-18 says:

> Then the Lord saw that the wickedness of man was great on the earth, and that every intent of the thoughts of his heart was only evil continually. And the Lord was sorry that He had made man on the earth, and He grieved in His heart. And the Lord said, "I will blot out man whom I have created from the face of the land, from man to animals to creeping things and to birds of the sky; for I am sorry that I have made them." But Noah found favor in the eyes of the Lord....

> "Make for yourself an ark.... I am bringing a flood of water upon the earth, to destroy all flesh in which is the breath of life... but I will establish My covenant with you" (NASB).

It is important to recognize that the flood of the Bible came about as the consequence of God's judgment, not as a natural disaster. Evolution minimizes the importance of the flood when it claims that there were only smaller local floods rather than one of catastrophic proportions.

Before the flood, God sent two of every kind of bird and animal to the ark so that they might procreate in the new world (Genesis 6:20). (Dinosaurs are perceived as enormous creatures but young dinosaurs are smaller and would probably have been the creatures God led to the ark.) Then God's judgment destroyed every living thing on earth. Sealed with a promise and a rainbow, a fresh start in a new world marked a new relationship between God and man. God gave Noah a command, "Be fruitful, and multiply, and replenish the earth (Genesis 9:1). The animals and man were told to scatter and fill the whole earth with life again.

Tragically, it didn't take man long to gain independence from God once more. Genesis 11 describes man's desire to reject God's mandates. Instead of scattering to the ends of the earth as God requested, he built a structure of worship and politics in order to "make for ourselves a name."

The men of Shinar, also known as the ancient city of Babylon, began constructing a city and tower, "whose top may reach unto heaven" (Genesis 11:1-4). Through their consolidation of might and brainpower they imagined themselves able to resist God. They stubbornly persisted with their plan "lest we be scattered abroad over the face of the whole earth." The futility of their suppositions brought about God's rapid judgment. He confused their language and scattered them abroad everywhere. Archeological discoveries show that even after God's dispersion, man continued to build such temples, or ziggurats, "of burned bricks" to other deities.

A Matter of Life and Death

Evolution not only robs God of His glory in creating life, it also destroys God's purpose of death and God's plan to overcome it through the resurrection of Jesus. The Bible says, "For the wages of sin is death"(Romans 6:23) and "Whoever believes may in Him [Jesus] have eternal life" (John 3:15 NASB).

Contrary to the abrupt formation of each species as stated in the Bible's creation story, evolution teaches that through the cycle of death came higher forms of life. Through endless cycles of death in one celled organisms came simple life. From the death of simple life came the formation of more complex life. Finally, through the death of apes came man. Evolution proposes that death combined with the survival of the fittest of a species is the mechanism which produces new and greater forms of life.

This philosophy is cousin to the concept of reincarnation, which is rooted in the pagan religions of the East. Reincarnation states that death and life are intrinsically joined together. They link arms with another cousin, suffering (known as "karma" in India), which is seen as the result of negative acts performed in this or other lifetimes. Such a concept is in contradiction to the view of abrupt appearance or creation by God, and ultimately of resurrection.

The Bible clearly describes the first death in Genesis 3. God killed an animal to provide a covering for Adam and Eve's sin, as a type of the shedding of blood for salvation that would occur when Jesus the Messiah died to provide eternal life. In Scripture death came about as a result of sin, not as an evolutionary mechanism by which simple life was transformed into more complex forms. To believe such a premise destroys the very heart of biblical Christianity. To cancel out and nullify the purpose of death and the atonement through the shedding of blood utterly contradicts God's plan and purpose.

Genesis develops the theme of atonement. The Jews were told continually to offer animal sacrifices to God with thanksgiving. Noah carried extra animals on the Ark to thank God for saving them. When the angel of death passed over the Egyptians homes and killed the firstborn sons in judgment for Pharaoh's rebellion against God, those Jews who had the blood of an unblemished lamb painted on their front portals were bypassed. Their lives were spared so that they could later enter the Promised Land. The sacrifice of an unblemished lamb illustrates the purpose and necessity of God's Messiah, Jesus described as "the lamb of God who takes away the sin of the world" (John 1:29) and is a fulfillment of Isaiah 53 prophecy.

Like the Jews who were bypassed by the angel of death, sinners today can be spared the ramifications of death only if they are covered by the blood of the Lamb, Jesus Christ. If man repents of his disobedience and rebellion against God and accepts Jesus, God's only salvation, God will forgive and forget man's sin—it's His promise.

What does all this have to do with evolution? Here's what G. Richard Bozarth, atheist and outspoken opponent of creationism, has said:

> Christianity has fought, still fights, and will fight science to the desperate end over evolution, because evolution destroys utterly and finally

the very reason Jesus' earthly life was supposedly made necessary. Destroy Adam and Eve and the original sin, and in the rubble you will find the sorry remains of the son of god. Take away the meaning of his death. If Jesus was not the redeemer who died for our sins, and this is what evolution means, then Christianity is nothing![1]

Bozarth's statement makes it apparent that atheism's agenda is to advance evolution and destroy the very foundational principles of biblical Christianity.

Holding Firm to the Faith

In the first epistle of Paul to Timothy, Paul urges Timothy to "instruct certain men not to teach strange doctrines, nor to pay attention to myths and endless genealogies, which give rise to mere speculation rather than furthering the administration of God which is by faith" (1:3,4 NASB).

Paul's warning could be applied to today's evolutionists who perpetuate strange myths and endless genealogies of man's descent from amoeba, lizards, and frogs to birds, dinosaurs, and apes. Paul's statement should also be assigned to many of today's Christians who have been duped by the many speculations of science.

The "strange doctrines" that Paul warned Timothy about were in fact the gnostic notions permeating the day's mindset. Greek teaching of the day was known as "demiurge" and became the first heresy of the church. It stated that creation emanated from a divine center, and that the original created a creature who created another, who created another, and so on. This reasoning concluded that Jesus, too, was just another created creature.

Paul's ability to stand against the philosophies of the day and aggressively teach the foundations of God was based on his superb grounding in the Holy Scriptures. Christians desiring to "fight the good fight" today would do well to learn from Paul. In order to "further the administration of God by faith," they should cling to the basics and cultivate a working knowledge of Scripture.

The Berean Jews, we are told in Acts 17:11, "were more noble-minded than those in Thessalonica [Greece], for they received the word with great eagerness, examining the Scriptures daily, to see whether these things were so."

When Paul spoke to the Jews about Jesus Christ he started from the foundation of their Scriptures, knowing that they had been grounded in Genesis. Jewish spirituality rested on the Hebrew Scriptures, which included the Genesis account of creation and God's promise to give His chosen people a Messiah. Paul had only to lead them through the Scriptures to introduce them to their Messiah, Jesus Christ.

But when Paul evangelized the Gentiles, he started from the evidence of creation itself. He knew that their worldview was heathen, that they came from pagan backgrounds and were unfamiliar with basic Jewish concepts. He knew of their myths and fables, and that their belief in the origins of life were grounded in Oriental mysticism. He was fully aware of the gnostic influence of the day. Christians today would do well to note Paul's strategy when introducing people to Christianity. Many who have been raised by the public school system and in non-Christian homes have been indoctrinated by evolutionary propaganda. They have not been exposed to credible information and scientific data that confirms the biblical view of creation.

God's Vengeful Adversary

In the beginning of the Bible we see the first of many examples of Satan's hatred toward God. His warfare is directly aimed at God, who alone has the power to overcome Satan. And the blessed assurance is that in His time, God ultimately will do so.

Meanwhile, Satan is out to destroy and kill what is pleasing to God. Because Christians, as believers in His Son, Jesus Christ, are pleasing to God and made in God's image, Satan's strategy is to weaken them. Satan wants to make life miserable for those who love God and who were intended to enjoy life on earth in fellowship with God.

We learn from Genesis that God gave Adam and Eve everything good. However He said, "Of every tree of the garden thou mayest freely eat: but of the tree of the knowledge of good and evil, thou shalt not eat of it: for in the day that thou eatest thereof thou shalt surely die" (2:16,17).

God loved His first people and they gave Him great pleasure. Satan's unquenchable jealousy caused him to compete with God for man's love. He sought to destroy the most perfect of relationships, Adam and Eve's harmony and agreement with their Creator.

Satan beguiled Eve to doubt God's love for her by implying that if God loved her, He would have let her eat from the restricted tree. Like today's evolutionists, Eve began to doubt that God's word was to be taken literally, and then she added to it.

Eve chose to believe that she had the ability to gain power and wisdom outside of conformity to God's law. She was deceived into thinking that she could manipulate and ultimately control her own life. Because of this willful decision, she and her husband were banished from their beautiful home. What was the importance of sending them away from the garden of Eden? What else could be disrupted if they were permitted to stay?

Chapter 3 states that there was another tree in the garden that had the potential for more abuse. In verses 22-24, we see the trinity in conversation saying, "Behold, the man is become as one of us, to know good and evil: and now, lest he put forth his hand, and take also of the tree of life, and eat, and live forever: Therefore the Lord God sent him forth from the garden of Eden . . . and he placed at the east of the garden of Eden Cherubims, and a flaming sword which turned every way, to keep the way of the tree of life."

God did not want man to live in sin and separation from Him for all eternity. In the state of rebellion that Adam and Eve were in, Satan may well have been able to seduce them to stay in bondage to him forever, without the freedom of God's provision of sacrifice.

Satan convinced Eve in the garden "Ye shall not surely die" (Genesis 3:4). This deceitful masterplanner continues to convince today's evolutionists that man's physical death has no spiritual sting or everlasting consequence. But the truth is that Satan has no power to release man from "the wages of sin [which] is death." Nor would he wish to.

God in his mercy made provision for sinful man's weakness. His solution was to save them through the sacrifice of His own innocent Son. He would wash away their iniquity through the blood of His Worthy Lamb!

Today, as in the garden, Satan continues to say that man is of no worth to God and is unloved by Him. Scripture, on the other hand, assures us that we can be lifted out of eternal despair if we make a choice to believe in Jesus' sacrifice for our sins. But alas, Satan's hold on man's mind and will continues with stubborn persistence.

Parenting in a Deceptive Age

Deuteronomy 6:7 provides special warning and instruction for parenting in the face of Satan's treacherous plans. Parents are to faithfully teach God's edicts and testimonies: "Thou shalt teach them [God's testimonies] diligently unto thy children, and shalt talk of them when thou sittest in thine house, and when thou walkest by the way, and when thou liest down, and when thou risest up." That command implies that we must always talk to our children, at all times of the day and evening, about the ways of the Lord. About His creation. About His power to create. About His purpose for creation. About His judgment when man disobeys. About His salvation through Jesus Christ.

The idea of constantly teaching our children from God's Word has been smothered by the accepted normalcy of sending our children to public schools, which are heavily influenced by humanism. Satan has largely gained control over the spiritual program of operation in our public schools. Christian prayer and traditional values are not allowed, but schools openly promote pagan worship and ideals from humanism, secularism, and other world religions. They do not allow the teaching of creation as a credible model for origins but perpetuate the lie of evolution as fact. They destroy family relationships by many times placing themselves above parents as authorities over children. In not supporting the principles of the Judeo-Christian tradition they stand against it and propagate an anti-God religion which forms a powerful part of the evolution conspiracy.

Satan already possesses the minds and souls of thousands of public-school children who are ensnared in his fables, and the results are devastating to their lives. In the next chapter we will see how the enemy's lies have become so deeply entrenched in our public school system.

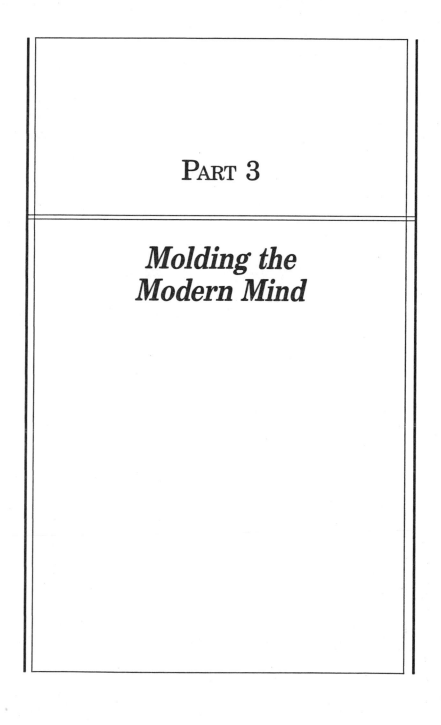

PART 3

Molding the Modern Mind

CHAPTER 8

Children at Risk

Traditionally the schoolroom has been an open forum of learning. Today it has become a pulpit for the aggressive conversion of impressionable minds. It is the battlefield where war is being waged against the Judeo-Christian God, His principles, His morality, and the Bible.

At a 1973 seminar on childhood education attended by 2,000 educators, Dr. Chester Pierce, a professor of education and psychiatry at Harvard University, said:

> Every child in America entering school at the age of five is mentally ill, because he comes to school with certain allegiances toward our founding fathers, toward our elected officials, toward his parents, toward a belief in a supernatural Being, toward the sovereignty of this nation as a separate entity. It's up to you teachers to make all of these sick children well by creating the international children of the future.[1]

Creeping into the Schools

The acceptance of the evolutionary doctrine following

the publication of Darwin's *Origin* in 1859 soon spread throughout the academic world in spite of the opposition of many scientists and religious leaders concerned about the validity of the new theory.

In parts of the industrialized world, controversy arose over whether the theory should be taught in schools. Many people would not accept the theory of evolution because it conflicted with their belief in God as the creator and sustainer of life. The Bible also made it clear that human beings were created in the image of God, and thus were elevated above all other forms of life. Because the majority of Americans still held this view, the teaching of evolution in this nation's public schools occurred gradually over many years.

The Scopes Trial

Between 1921 and 1929, anti-evolution bills were brought before 37 American state legislatures. The bills were designed to outlaw the teaching of all but the biblical doctrine of creation in the public schools and colleges.

The first major confrontation with these laws occurred at the famous Scopes Trial, which took place in 1925. John T. Scopes of Dayton, Tennessee, was tried for teaching evolution in violation of a Tennessee anti-evolution law which had been passed earlier that year. He lost and the repercussions of the trial on education were felt for many years. Most schools avoided teaching evolution, and publishers produced texts that barely touched the topic.[2]

Humanism Joins the Evolution Conspiracy

The year 1933 marked a major milestone along the pathway for establishing evolutionary teaching in the classroom. During that pivotal year 34 individuals constructed and signed a document called the Humanist Manifesto. This text laid out a number of philosophical and religious principles.

The main objective of the Humanist Manifesto was to redirect the thinking of society. The manifesto represented man's effort to solve his problems and shape his society apart from God. The official creed began, "The time has come for widespread recognition of the radical changes in beliefs throughout the modern world."[3]

A worldview based on old ideas, especially biblical concepts, was attacked and ridiculed:

> The time is past for mere revision of traditional attitudes. Science and economic change have disrupted the old beliefs. Religions the world over are under the necessity of coming to terms with the new conditions created by a vastly increased knowledge and experience."[4]

A new "vision" for the future was projected that would provide meaning and direction to human life. That vision was based on the establishment of the religion of humanism.

> While this age does owe a vast debt to traditional religions, it is none the less obvious that any religion that can hope to be a synthesizing and dynamic force for today must be shaped for the needs of this age. To establish such a religion is a major necessity of the present. It is a responsibility which rests upon this generation.[5]

With this document, the signers of the Humanist Manifesto made their intentions clear. Because humanism is based on evolutionary principles, the Humanist Manifesto thrust the creation/evolution issue into the forefront of public awareness. Its two primary tenets were:

> First: Religious humanists regard the universe as self-existing and not created.
>
> Second: Humanism believes that man is a part of nature and that he has emerged as a result of a continuous process.[6]

The chief designer of the 1933 Humanist Manifesto was John Dewey. An honorary president of the National Education Association, Dewey became one of the major driving forces for the spread of the humanistic message throughout public education in the twentieth century.[7]

Dewey was a committed atheist and an active member of the American Humanist Association. He claimed that it was useless to teach children any moral absolutes. He felt that fixed moral laws and eternal truths were outdated and restrictive. He believed that truth was relative and believing in God and a biblical view of creation was not admissible. Dewey had a passion to see the evolutionary theory taught in the classroom[8] and championed its cause, even though it took another two decades before evolution was actively implemented into public schools.

Another important supporter and signer of this document was Charles Francis Potter. Potter was also an honorary president of the National Education Association. In 1930 he wrote a book called *Humanism: A New Religion*, in which he laid out the objective of his religion of humanism that leaves little to the imagination:

> Education is thus a most powerful ally of Humanism, and every American public school is

a school of Humanism. What can a theistic Sunday school's meeting, for an hour once a week and teaching only a fraction of the children, do to stem the tide of the five day program of humanistic teaching?[9]

So it was that the godless religion of humanism based on the principle of evolution began. Humanism joined the evolution conspiracy forcefully and intentionally. It recognized that the most fertile ground for the advancement of its goals was our educational system.

When evolution and humanism fused, the stakes in the battle to legitimize evolution rose. Humanists knew that in order to turn people from God, they needed to find an alternate explanation to satisfy man's innate desire to know where he came from. Evolution provided that explanation, and its unholy alliance with humanism has become one of the guiding principles of education.

Humanism Updated

In September of 1973, the American Humanist Association, acting jointly with the American Ethical Union, released the final text of an updated version of the Humanist Manifesto. Over 260 prominent individuals from all over the world who despised biblical concepts signed this document.[10] Humanist Manifesto II reinforces the humanist objective to replace a belief in God with the religion of worshiping man. The idea of a prayer-hearing God is said to be an "unapproved and outmoded faith."[11]

According to Humanist Manifesto II, humanism offers an alternative that will serve present needs and guide mankind toward the future. The common theme of the manifesto is "to design a *secular* society on a *planetary* scale (emphasis added)," an idea that will become increasingly important in later chapters. Looking toward the future the declaration said, "While there is much we do not know, humans are responsible for what we are or what we will become. No deity will save us; we must save ourselves."[12]

Evolutionary Advances in the Classroom

The melding of humanism and evolutionism in our educational system came about gradually as more and more influential educators embraced the concepts. The issue of whether or not evolution should be taught in the classroom remained relatively dormant until the 1950's, at which time concern that science courses in the public schools needed to be upgraded opened a window of opportunity for evolutionists. The Soviet Union had just launched its first Sputnik, and U.S. scientists realized that America could soon fall behind in science and technology if they didn't improve the quality of the science education from the grade-school level upward.[13]

In the 1960's, a group of biologists received a grant from the National Science Foundation to revamp high school biology curriculum. The Biological Sciences Curriculum Study group, (BSCS) produced a series of science textbooks using evolution as the major unifying theme. The books that BSCS produced were widely accepted, and by the 1970's over half of the students taking high school biology in North America were using these materials.[14]

Ten years later a social science curriculum called "Man: A Course of Study" (MACOS) was initiated. Another project of the National Science Foundation, the fifth- and sixth-grade course was designed to show a comparative study of animal and human behavior. By 1974, 1700 school districts in 47 states had adopted MACOS.[15]

The reappearance of evolution in school textbooks elicited a strong reaction from people who clung to the biblical view of creationism. Vigorous resistance was communicated to school boards and government legislators, demanding that evolution be banned from the classroom. Some protesters argued that the teaching of evolution in schools in the United States was against the law. However, when the issue was brought before the U.S. Supreme Court in 1968, the court ruled that banning the teaching of evolution would be unconstitutional because doing so would favor one particular religious viewpoint over others.[16]

The Creationism Movement

Unable to sit back and allow the new wave of evolutionary and humanistic dogma to spread unchallenged throughout the North American continent, a move toward presenting the alternative view of creationism *alongside* evolution in classrooms began to develop. Concerned about the way evolution was being presented as fact, a growing number of organizations throughout the United States and Canada began to find their voice.

In 1972, a center called the Institute for Creation Research (ICR) was established in El Cajon, California. Along with a staff of several professional scientists with advanced degrees in engineering and science, Dr. Henry Morris formed an organization that quickly began to impact the world. ICR's objective was to make the Christian church, as well as the general public, aware of the physical evidence which confirms the biblical record and contradicts the evolutionary view.

Numerous other groups and individuals felt the same urgency to present a similar message to the church and general public. Over the next several years the creationism movement began to spread throughout the country. Debates were held on college campuses throughout America. Experts such as Dr. Morris and Dr. Duane Gish of ICR pointed out some of the fallacies of the evolution view. Books, magazines, pamphlets, and other publications appeared in bookstores and libraries; seminar presentations were held in churches and public halls. In every way possible, creationists attempted to show that the biblical account of origins was a credible alternative to the theory of evolution. They maintained that both views should be presented side-by-side in the classroom.

Resistance to this approach was strong. As creationists persisted in making their viewpoint understood, the creation versus evolution controversy became remarkably widespread.

One of the main arguments against the presentation of creation in the secular classroom was the concern that the message would give support to the Bible. This, as we have already pointed out, would attack the establishment of the "secular society" which had been so clearly planned many years before by the designers of the original Humanist Manifesto. For those people firmly entrenched in humanist propaganda, the enemy which they had been called to fight was the narrow-minded and bigoted evangelical church which held firmly to a literal interpretation of the Bible. This made the creationist speakers a threat beyond measure:

> They bring "scientific creationism" to the public forum at every opportunity and are masters at convincing their audience that they have been

"duped" by the evolutionary establishment. The creationists love to appear scientific themselves and they enhance this illusion by their fluency in scientific jargon and terminology. They also write and debate with professional skill.[17]

According to one spokesman defending the credibility of evolution, another troublesome tactic of the pesky creationists was the way they deviously attacked the evolution theory: "The Creationists obtain most of their 'scientific' evidence against evolution by identifying facts which are 'inconvenient' to evolutionists—facts which are not easily explained in terms of evolution as it is presently understood."[18]

To the humanists, the greatest threat of all facing the advancement of education in America was the blatant way in which the creationist strategy seemed to bypass the scientific authorities and appeal to the general public. Willard Young describes the deplorable situation which he could see developing among creation "heretics":

A recourse commonly followed by heretics outside the scientific community, who are frustrated by their inability to have the community recognize their ideas, is to bypass scientists and appeal to the general public. There are always enough people among the general public who have little or no comprehension of the scientific issues, that the heretic may gain a sympathetic following.

Not only does this bolster the confidence and the ego of the heretic, but the publicity may eventually drive scientists to respond publically as well. If this happens, the heretic will have finally succeeded in getting the attention of scientists, but in an environment which does not recognize, or even rejects, the intellectual standards and criteria of proof which the philosophy of science demands. Scientists are then faced with the difficulty of defending the scientific position in an unscientific context to people with little or no real understanding of science.[19]

Obviously the creationist movement was a troublesome barrier to the furthering of the theory of evolution and to the establishment of the priesthood called science that was such an essential part of the humanists' "new secular society." Certainly there was a lot of pride at stake if the lowly masses made up of scientific illiterates were allowed to be indoctrinated by such "heresy" as creationism.

The Threat to Humanism

In the early 1980's Wayne Moyer, an executive director for the National Association for Biology Teachers, aired his concern for what he termed "the challenge of creationism." Moyer sternly addressed his colleagues:

How many scientists are aware that an extensive press, supported by and directed to religious fundamentalists, consistently teaches biblical creationism? Or the multi-million dollar TV and radio network featuring evangelistic preaching, hymns and money raising, which takes the same position? Or that well funded organizations like the Institute For Creation Research [ICR], with a reported annual budget in excess of a half a million dollars, devote their efforts solely toward

denigrating evolution while proselytizing creationism? Or that highly polished and persuasive
speakers appear regularly on college campuses,
either to debate scientists in a no-win set-up, or
to speak on creationism?[20]

Moyer, after attempting to awaken his colleagues from
their complacency, added further fuel to the fire:

For creationists the overriding issue is human
origin: Have we ascended from the beasts or were
we divinely created in God's image? If the former
is accepted by their children attending public
schools, the fundamentalists' entire doctrinal
position is badly shaken if not destroyed. Far
better then [for the Christian] to force creationist doctrine into the biology curriculum, thereby
neutralizing their children's exposure to instruction in evolution.[21]

Moyer was not the first individual to make such a statement. Less than two years earlier, in an article in *The
American Atheist*, Richard Bozarth had written about the
importance of creation to the Christian perspective. "Even
a high school student knows enough about evolution to
know that nowhere in the evolutionary description of our
origins does there appear an Adam or an Eve or an Eden or
a forbidden fruit," he said.[22]

Bozarth then challenged his fellow atheists to take up
the cause, rise to the occasion, and destroy Christianity:

Christianity, if it is to survive, must have an
Adam and the original sin and the fall from
grace, or it can not have Jesus the redeemer who

restores to those who believe what Adam's disobedience took away. What this all means is that Christianity cannot lose the Genesis account of creation.... The battle must be waged, for Christianity is fighting for its very life.[23]

Fanning the Flames

Isaac Asimov, without question one of the best-known names in the world associated with the field of science is a dedicated atheist and a signer of Humanist Manifesto II.[24] Asimov has boasted: "I am an atheist, out and out. I don't have the evidence to prove God doesn't exist, but I so strongly suspect he does not that I don't want to waste my time."[25]

Obviously upset by the idea of allowing students in the classroom the opportunity to hear the creationist position, Asimov argued: "Creationists don't want equal time. They want all the time there is."[26]

Such exasperation with the creationists necessitated a call for action from the prominent Asimov, especially in light of the fact that fulfillment of Humanist Manifesto II, which he so proudly signed, would be in jeopardy should the creation movement continue unhindered. Asimov sent out a long fund-appeal letter for the American Civil Liberties Union (ACLU) urging people to send money to help the ACLU fight creationism wherever it appeared.[27] The ACLU is the self-appointed legal arm of secular humanism and a strong opponent of creation being presented as an alternative to evolution in public schools.

Pesky Creationists

Science *was* being challenged, as Wayne Moyer stated in his editorial called "The Challenge of Creationism."[28] He made a number of observations and predictions which warned that the dangers of creationism were just beginning. If the movement continued unchecked, textbook publishers would be forced to "reduce evolutionary concepts and include scientific creationism"; creationist pressure could "eliminate funding of projects incorporating evolutionary concepts"; and scientists and their "methods of science" would increasingly come under attack.[29]

The time had come for a consolidation of forces.

CHAPTER 9

Onward Evolutionary Soldiers

Evolutionary theory has been enshrined as the centerpiece of our educational system, and elaborate walls have been erected around it to protect it from unnecessary abuse.[1]

—Jeremy Rifkin, author and New Age spokesperson

With such high profile science promoters as Isaac Asimov and Wayne Moyer calling for a coordinated effort designed to suppress the creation movement, and financed by the donations of concerned evolutionists, the battle cry had been sounded.

No longer could evolutionists allow the growing threat of state laws mandating the teaching of creationism in secular schools to continue. The time was ripe for a wholesale reaction by evolutionists and their supporters.

Two separate meetings, October 19 and 20, 1981 signaled the beginnings of such a reaction.[2] The first meeting was organized by the National Academy of Sciences (NAS), an organization representing the scientific profession and designated adviser to the U.S. government in matters of science.[3] The second meeting was held by the National Association of Biology Teachers (NABT). Over the two days of meetings held in the nation's capital, the creation-evolution issue was discussed in great detail. Many top scientists and educators gathered to review the present seriousness of the situation and plan a strategy to attack the creation movement.

William Meyer, director of the Biological Sciences Curriculum Study (BSCS) was one of the first to speak to the NABT. His motivational speech set the mood for the conference: "The whole structure of science is under attack," he declared. "And it's not just biology that's in danger, it's all of science: geology, physics, astronomy. The creationists are attempting to mandate what is appropriate for study and what is not."[4]

Niles Eldridge, a curator at the American Museum of Natural History in New York then proclaimed to his shocked sympathizers: "The creationists have already made moves to secure funding for so-called creation science on an equal footing with evolution science. This should be sufficient to convince my colleagues that the house is really on fire."[5]

The participants of the meetings were ready to make plans for the future. Members of the NAS group suggested that a good way to make people more aware of evolution would be to assemble some basic facts about evolution and put them in a short, simple, and visually attractive presentation.[6]

It was recommended that a booklet be put together by the NAS and distributed to school teachers and others on the front line, so that they would be better equipped to argue the case for evolution.

Others commented on the need to produce books, termed "manuals of intellectual self defense,"[7] attacking the creation premise.

In fact it was generally agreed that not all evolutionists were prepared to answer the creationist arguments. The NABT suggested that what was needed was "a handy creation refuter." After all, it was pointed out, the creationists have a "handy dandy evolution refuter" (a small booklet by that name written by a creationist, which points out the many fallacies of evolution). Another spokesperson agreed: "We have to ensure that teachers and college professors have appropriate information in pithy form so they can answer reporters' questions when the time comes."[8]

Stanley Weinberg, a retired biology teacher from Iowa stressed the need to set up a "network of committees of correspondence," throughout the United States, enabling local communities to react to the initiatives by the creationists. Such a highly coordinated system would provide names of people who could respond authoritatively, assemble resources to fight the creationists, and monitor information which would trace the activity of the creationist movement.

Further recommendations included the provision of resources for a small number of accomplished speakers who could lecture throughout the country, and even the possibility that the president of NAS could devote substantial effort to expose the nature of the problem through "influential channels."[9]

Dr. John Moore, veteran anticreationist from the University of California (Riverside) summed up what he felt was at the heart of the creation-evolution issue. With an altar call that would challenge the sincerity of any genuine humanist supporter, Dr. Moore challenged his listeners: "If we do not resolve our problems with the creationists, we have only ourselves to blame. Let us remember, the greatest resource of all is available to us—the educational system of the nation."[10]

Defending the Evolutionary Faith

The October summit fired up many of the world's most dedicated evolution supporters with a desire to obliterate creation from the classroom and push onward for the advancement of science. For many, it was an insult to the realm of human intelligence that the theory of evolution had come under attack.

It was almost inconceivable that scientists and educators dedicated to the advancement of understanding, would have to divert their attention to attack such "pseudo-scientific heresy" as creationism.

Many agreed that the strength of the creationist movement centered on small groups of sincere, energetic, and zealous believers all over North America. In supporting creationism and undermining evolution, these groups worked both formally and informally. The creation activists went to public meetings and made their voices heard. They organized meetings of their own. They distributed literature and button-holed people. They rang doorbells, sent letters, and called in to talk shows. They lobbied legislators and other public officials. In fact creationists, it was accused, had even intimidated teachers in the public school system, so that rather than teaching "creationism and evolution," they would teach neither one.[11]

And so a revitalized, insulted, but proud army of evolutionist soldiers went out to battle with a vengeance they had never had before. From October 1981 on, they began to write, sponsor, issue, and support publications attacking creation. They developed pro-evolution publicity through the press and the electronic media. They testified before legislative committees, school boards, and textbook committees. They held and participated in meetings and debates.

It didn't take long before a barrage of anticreation publications started appearing on the newsstands and in bookstores. One of the first books to launch the attack was *Science on Trial, the Case for Evolution*, by Douglas Futyma.[12] The preface of Futyma's book begins where the Washington summit for the promotion of evolution left off.

According to Futyma, Christian fundamentalists were at the very root of degrading science by placing it "on trial." But people might logically ask why it should bother evolutionists to be on trial if the proof for evolution exists.

In his first chapter, "Reason Under Fire," Futyma expresses his consternation. How is it possible he questions, in an age "when we have sent spacecraft past Saturn, discovered the forces that move continents and lift mountains, traced the biochemical pathway of the cell, and revealed the molecular structure of the gene, that science should still be at war with the remnants of medieval theology"? He then warns his readers of the serious attack which is taking place against evolution, headed up by fundamentalist Christians who have "passed laws," "attacked museums," "assaulted biology, physics, astronomy, geology anthropology and psychology,"and are attempting to "extinguish secular humanism."[13]

What angers Futyma and other anticreationists is the success which the creationists have had in advancing their message. Among the reasons for their success, Futyma suggests that creationism appeals to a special class of people: "they offer simple, unambiguous, and certain answers to those who cannot live with complexity, ambiguity, and uncertainty."[14]

He also notes that the creationists are able to brainwash these so-called scientific illiterates by presenting "an appealingly black-and-white caricature of science that makes few demands on its audience's intellect."[15] Not only was the credibility of evolution being undermined by creationists, but the pride of many highly educated and trained devotees was also at stake.

Mass Mailings

The National Academy of Sciences was also active in its role to build up public confidence in the cherished theory of evolution. In an interview for the film *The Evolution Conspiracy,* Dr. Preston Cloud, Director of Geological Science at University of California (Berkeley) and a spokesman for the NAS, explained what took place following the October 1981 meeting in Washington:

> As the creationists became more active, some of us in the academy became more and more concerned with the legal activities that were attempting to force this religious issue in the classroom. Eventually, the academy resolved that it must have a committee to review and decide what could be done about it, and the result of that was an organization of a committee of Science and Creationism.[16]

The Science and Creationism committee did not waste time in taking action. During February 1984, the first copies of a booklet called "Science and Creationism, A View from the National Academy of Sciences"[17] rolled off the press. The attractive 28-page color brochure was exactly what had been recommended. Frank Press, president of NAS, outlined why the booklet had been prepared: "The teaching of the scientific theory of evolution alongside creationism is inappropriate."[18] He stated further that the theory of evolution had "successfully withstood the tests of science many, many times."[19]

More than 40,000 copies of this booklet were mailed out by the NAS all over the United States. They were sent to school district superintendents and secondary school science department heads, as well as to organizations such as the National Science Teachers Association. According to a letter which was sent along with the NAS booklet, the special publication dedicated to the demise of the creation movement was also sent to selected members of the U.S. Congress,[20] perhaps partially fulfilling the recommendation to approach the creation-evolution issue through "influential channels" that had been suggested earlier.[21]

But books and publications written to those directly related to the field of science and science education were not the only way the evolutionary humanists were making their case known. Countless magazine articles were targeted to the average layperson, warning the apathetic public of the critical need to destroy creationism.

Bob Guccione, editor-in-chief of *Omni* magazine, considered the threat of the creationists so severe that in February 1987 he dedicated almost the entire issue to exposing the creation-evolution controversy and the subject of "Science and Censorship."[22]

Kathleen Stein, *Omni* staff writer, set the mood for her article called "Censoring Science" by expressing personal feelings about creationists and the creationist movement. In her remarks she briefs the reading audience of the threat that creationists pose as they allegedly "censor science education" and "reject the theory of evolution as heresy." Then comes a warning: "I've investigated some really exciting scientific research, and I thought creationists' efforts were a joke, a surreal dream. But after meeting these people, I viewed it much more seriously and it frightens me."[23]

On page 22 of the same magazine, author Harlan Ellison comments on the subject of science and censorship, an evil for which creationists have been accused, and makes the following observations: "These would-be censors are monsters. And they will always be with us because the two most common things in the universe are hydrogen and stupidity." Addressing the situation further he said, "Anyone who deludes him or herself thinking that these people are not the biggest danger we face—on the level of our day to day lives—is living in la-la land. We may survive the military-industrial complex—I am convinced we won't have a nuclear war—but we can never survive these people who seek to drive us back to the Dark Ages."

The growing hostility toward the creationist position was brought into clear focus in this issue of *Omni* as readers were challenged to make a response by detaching a postcard, signing the card, and mailing it to the President of the United States. The card stated:

> I violently oppose censorship in any form and protest the recent attempts by right wing religious zealots aided and abetted by elements of your own administration to infringe upon my First Amendment right. Current efforts to ban textbooks on evolution and other bona fide aspects of biology are especially repugnant. If such efforts are allowed to succeed, American education will recede into the Dark Ages, and our children will grow up severely handicapped, unable to compete with the children of other technologically advanced societies.

Revealing Polls

In spite of the confident position taken by scientists and educators regarding the absolute "fact of evolution," opinion surveys in the 80's revealed that the general public was still not as firmly convinced. A national Gallup survey conducted in 1982 revealed:

> 44% of Americans said they believed "God created man pretty much in his present form within the last several thousand years."

> 38% believed "man had developed over millions of years from a less advanced form of life, but God guided this process, including man's creation."

> 9% believed "man had developed over millions of years from lower forms of life, without God having any part in the process."

> 9% held some other belief or did not have any opinion.

When the respondents were asked which version should be taught in the schools:

> 38% said creationism

> 33% said evolutionism with God in control

> 9% said evolution without God

> 4% volunteered "all three"

> 4% volunteered "none"

> 12% fell into the "other/don't know" category.[24]

Only 9 percent of the respondents felt that evolution without God should be taught in the schools, yet a small band of humanistic educators and scientists continued to gain power to dictate our educational destiny.

Open and unwarranted hostility toward creationism was represented by another short article appearing in *Discover* magazine under the derogatory title, "Ignorance 101." It revealed that nearly 45 percent of those surveyed (2,100 students at 41 U.S. colleges and universities) said they believed fossils were the remains of animals that died in the flood; 38 percent believed man originated in the garden of Eden; and nearly 10 percent (from the south) believed that earth was created less than 6,000 years ago. Fifty-two percent of the students surveyed from the southwest believed that "the origin of human life is best explained by creation by God as in Genesis."

"I was surprised by the general level of naivete," says University of California at San Francisco psychiatrist John Cronin, "because college students can presumably think through certain issues."[25]

Another well-known anticreationist and dedicated supporter of the evolutionary doctrine is Dr. Vincent Sarich, professor at the University of California at Berkeley. During an interview for the film *The Evolution Conspiracy*, Dr. Sarich expressed the need to reprogram the masses with scientific truth.

> The fact is that most people are creationists of one kind or another. Most people are not evolutionists; most people do not believe that evolution happened. The fact that most scientists do, or practically all scientists do, is in a sense neither here nor there, because in fact, we would like the ideas to get across to our students. We

have to remember that creationism was what everybody thought not all that many years ago. And creationism was overthrown in the scientific community by evolutionary thinking.[26]

Over the past several decades, the realm of education has made every possible attempt to indoctrinate the general public with "the fact of evolution." From kindergarten through elementary education, children are told about the process which randomly directs nonliving material to become life. And for those who continue on into higher levels of education such as universities and colleges, more specific details are added. All of this, as we have seen, furthers the conspiracy to oust the God of creation from His rightful place:

> The battle for humankind's future must be waged and won in the public school classroom.... The classroom must and will become an arena of conflict between the old and the new—the rotting corpse of Christianity ... and the new faith of Humanism.[27]

Legal Challenges to Creationism

As a result of the concerted effort of humanists and evolutionists, the academic freedom of thousands of schoolchildren is being thwarted daily because the whole story of life's origins isn't presented. Half the story is censored! It seems criminal that tax dollars which are put into public schools, museums, and national and state parks contribute to the circulation of a controlled educational bias. This limitation opposes most people's desire for fair and equal representation of both theories.

In 1981 Louisiana passed a law for balanced treatment of creation science (defined as "scientific evidence") and evolution to be taught in schools. The ACLU immediately threatened to file suit. It argued that Louisiana's law violated separation of church and state as well as academic freedom.

Wendell Bird, the attorney who was asked to defend the state of Louisiana against the ACLU's lawsuit, said, "To me, the basic issue is academic freedom because no one is trying to exclude evolution from public schools while teaching a theory of creation. Instead, the evolutionists are trying to exclude alternatives, while in general defending the exclusive teaching of evolution."[28]

Does a balanced treatment for creation science and evolution constitute a violation of church and state? A two-sided approach seems to be a very fair request. But it provokes seemingly irrational antagonism from those who are committed to the exclusive teaching of evolution. They firmly insist on barring the scientific theory of creation and abrupt appearance.

Bird says, "That's censorship in my view! That's defending indoctrination while opposing alternative views, trying to preserve the favorite viewpoint and to exclude the others... The Supreme Court specifically said, 'teaching a variety of scientific theories about the origins of human-kind to school children might be validly done with clear secular intent and enhancing the effect of science instruction.' In two other places the majority opinion referred to teachers already possessing a flexibility to supplement the present science curriculum with the presentation of theories besides evolution about the origin of life."[29]

In other words, the United States Supreme Court has ruled that it is permissible to teach all of the scientific evidence on origins. Yet this important decision has been overruled already in the state of California. How long will it be before our entire nation loses all freedom to teach provable, factual information about creation?

Harassment Toward Creationism

The movement to aggressively advance evolutionism which was begun in the early 1980's birthed the introduction of "Science Framework for California Public Schools." On January 13, 1989 the State Board of Education issued its policy on the teaching of natural science. The objective of the policy is to upgrade science by advancing evolutionism and eliminating any reference to a Creator. The teaching of evolutionism was said to be appropriate to the science classroom while "divine creation" was relegated to the history-social science and English-language arts curricula.[30]

"Nothing in science or in any other field of knowledge shall be taught dogmatically," says the report. "A dogma is a system of beliefs that is not subject to scientific test and refutation. Compelling belief is inconsistent with the goal of education." Interestingly, while such an adamant statement is intended to criticize and curb creationism it highlights the weaknesses of evolutionary propagation, which is taught as "dogma" and is "not subject to scientific test." It is also a "compelling belief... inconsistent with the goal of education" as described by the State Board policy itself.[31]

The state is also extending it tentacles into private education. For example, The Institute for Creation Research (ICR) is a science graduate school that teaches science within a creationist framework. It receives no state or federal funding and yet has been continually harassed by California's Department of Education. After two years of threats, the Department of Education finally denied ICR the right to operate and offer Master of Science degrees. It claimed that ICR's "creationist framework did not measure up to academic standards normally demanded of a post-graduate institution."[32]

"It boils down to a truth-in-advertising issue," says William L. Rukeyser, special assistant to California Superintendent of Public Instruction. "If I'm selling a used car and I've got a Chevy, I can't call it a Ford. If ICR wants to teach about beliefs or religion, nobody is going to stand in their way. They just have to accurately label what they are teaching."[33] Yet if that reasoning were applied equally, the state would have to relabel its own evolutionary teaching as religion.

It becomes increasingly apparent that the attack on ICR is only the tip of the iceberg. It is not only private colleges like ICR but also private Christian schools that are in jeopardy of losing their constitutional freedom of religion and the academic freedom to decide their own curriculum.

Even teachers in public schools who teach within the constitutionally permissable framework of presenting all scientific evidence to teach the origins of life are at risk. This was demonstrated in a recent incident involving science teacher John Peloza, runner-up Teacher of the Year in 1990-91. Peloza was fired from his seven-year teaching position in Mission Viejo, California, for "presenting a theory of intelligent design along with evolution in his classroom."[34] The *Southern California Christian Times* reported that "the school district is forcing Peloza to teach evolution as dogma, and censoring him from presenting any scientific evidence that challenges the theory—a position which is a violation of Supreme Court ruling *Edwards v. Aguillard* in 1987."

The *Orange County Register* quoted Peloza as saying, "Evolution is a state-sponsored religion paid for by the taxpayers. I'm being pressured to proselytize [this religion] to my students."[35]

The significance of persecutions such as these is that the conspiracy to advance evolutionism has successfully gone beyond verbal intimidation to loss of jobs, academic license, and legal action. Those in power are exercising their supremacy beyond what is reasonable.

If the battle against censorship of the evidence for creationism is not waged, our children will continue to be influenced by evolutionists and humanists who are even now preparing the way for what they believe will be a brave new secular future and the next step in man's evolution—the quantum leap to godhood.

PART 4

The Global Search for Spirituality

CHAPTER 10

A Quantum Leap into the New Age

There is a clear but complex marriage between *physical* evolution and *transcendental* evolution. Ironically, while forcing out creationism, many scientists and educators push for an equally religious alternative. They cling to the Eastern concept that the next stage of man's evolution will arrive in spiritual terms. Many prophesy a development—a quantum leap from biological evolution into a sort of "mystical emergence."

Fritjof Capra, professor of physics at University of California (Berkeley) and prominent advocate of New Age thought, says, "The universe is no longer seen as a machine, made up of a multitude of objects, but has to be pictured as one indivisible, dynamic whole whose parts are essentially interrelated and can be understood only as patterns of a cosmic process."[1]

After so much indoctrination in and exposure to the unproven ideas of evolutionary thinking, growing numbers of people are now accepting the concept of this "cosmic process" as the most natural thing in the world. Natural, but deadly. For this blurring of physical and spiritual evolution thickens into a hot spiritual "porridge" made up of a variety of assorted "cereals." Mystical alchemy,

charading as spiritual evolution, combines with speculation about physical evolution. This fuses with "Eastern
maya," the belief that the physical (the real, what we see)
is merging with the not-yet-physical (maya), and that the
mind is able to create reality (shamanism, witchcraft).
This opens the door to every form of New Age deception.

The New Age movement is a hybrid of spiritually eclec-
tic pagan consciousness that embraces every idolatry named
in the Bible. Though it poses as a spiritually tolerant
mindset, it is extremely intolerant of biblical Christianity.

The philosophies under its umbrella are numerous. A
general summary would be any mental techniques involving altered states of consciousness through deep-breathing
relaxation exercises, guided imagery, and visualization. It
may also include the application of dietary or mystical
folklore promising power.

Interwoven into its philosophy are a proliferation of
Eastern religions such as Hinduism, Buddhism, and Taoism.
It includes guru movements, psychotherapy cults, aber-
rational Christian movements, blatant satanism, witchcraft, the practice of nature worship—and the list goes on.
Beliefs and practices that used to be considered overtly
heathen, rooted in pantheistic evolution and confined to
the streets of India or the Far East, are now common
practice in millions of homes across the USA and Europe.
(For further reading see *Gods of the New Age* and the
Recommended Reading list.)

Mysticism Goes Mainstream

In the February 1987 *American Health* magazine, an
article by Andrew Greenly entitled "Mysticism Goes Mainstream" includes the following subtitle: "New data shows
most Americans have experienced ESP or had contact

with the dead—and psychological tests show they may be better for it."

The article reveals how Eastern religious ideas and a belief in paranormal experiences have changed the nature of Western society. "Forty-two percent of American adults now believe they have been in contact with someone who has died" and "23 percent of Americans now believe in reincarnation according to pollster George Gallup, Jr."

Reincarnation, the close cousin of evolution, teaches that the human soul evolves to soaring heights from its animal beginnings. This essence (soul) is seen as a fragment of the "divine," which is purposed to eventually return to its divine source. It is inseparably linked to its larger part, the cosmos, which is also understood to be "divine."

Exponents of reincarnation believe that the soul must pass through recurring cycles of birth, life, death, and rebirth. Ultimately, depending on karma, the soul may or may not achieve "release," known as salvation. It is believed that one soul can travel through billions of years and just as many people.

In Hinduism, reincarnation is seen as a hopeless imprisonment! But in our society, the average person reads glamorized magazine articles on this comfortless concept at any variety of places—the doctor's office, the beauty salon, the supermarket, or in the growing New Age sections of bookstores across the nation. Those inclined to pursue their spiritual quest have an unending supply of books, tapes, videos, and classes available today. Or they can attend any of the hundreds of psychic fairs springing up across America and Europe.

Through the media and events such as psychic fairs people are exposed to every sort of New Age/occult paraphernalia—from crystals, astrological charts, and meditative techniques to holistic bodyworks and health products, intuitive arts, channelings (old-fashioned "demon possession"), and thousands of pieces of information on reincarnation and its parallel ideas maya, karma, and evolution.

One psychic fair, the "Whole Life Expo," claims to have drawn 50,000 people to its Los Angeles exhibition in 1987. Its owner and director, Paul Andrews, said in his interview for the film *The Evolution Conspiracy*, "I believe that the New Age movement is heading into the mainstream of American consciousness, and I think that it's going to get there by exposure in the mass media, the ideas, the concepts, the principles, the psychology, the spirituality, the inner-directed, searching, goal-oriented drive that people have to capture and be part of their higher self."

Finding the Higher Self

The road to one's "higher self" can be long and those who travel it may require a good deal of New Age healing along the way. Many New Age magazines advertise a myriad of these therapies and techniques. Such material is often given away at health food stores throughout America, and promotes transcendental meditation, yoga, psychic readers, astrology, visualization, and numerous other occultic practices.

Many modern health practitioners, including doctors and psychologists, have fallen under the spell of "holistic" medicine, a discipline in which the human body, mind, and spirit are recognized as a part of the cosmos at large. When one part of the body is ill, the healer will claim that the "spirit" must be treated by drawing on the manipulation of cosmic forces, powers, and energies. One example of how this has crossed over into the mainstream of society is that in England, old-age pensioners are now encouraged to practice Transcendental Meditation by National Health Care doctors.

Yoga, Eastern mediation, visualization, and other forms of hypnosis are designed to train the use of occult "energy" to escape from reality, pacify stress, and nullify ills. These notions are based on the unbiblical premise that mankind has the authority to alleviate all suffering through mind-altering techniques.

As for the feasibility of mind-altering techniques having the power to change reality, a recent *Los Angeles Times* article challenges this notion. The article tells of disenchantment across the United States with hospital classes that promote "natural childbirth" education. The purpose of such classes, primarily Lamaze, is to prepare mothers emotionally and physically for a relaxed and relatively painfree labor with little or no medication. Now almost 40 years after its introduction, Lamaze's breathing techniques have left mothers and hospital workers disillusioned because they "know it doesn't work." Along with most other natural childbirth classes, Lamaze is a philosophy that intends to teach clients that painfree childbirth *is* possible because "the huge majority of pain comes from your head." This concept is in direct opposition to the reality of pain acquired in giving birth that is a consequence of Eve's disobedience in the garden of Eden (Genesis 3:16). Confident Lamaze promoters, however, say "the technique has undergone necessary refinements":

> We're moving closer to understanding pain and how it's transmitted and how to interrupt it. We've gone to increased use of imagery and relaxation and are putting the emphasis less on breathing."[2]

Occult techniques which attempt to manipulate reality are akin to witchcraft and cannot override God's authority because we imagine they do.

Food for Thought

The holistic movement also embraces the idea that a system of psychic or "spiritual" accomplishments or tasks can lead a person along the path to higher evolution. Man credits himself with the facility of redemption, a power that only Jesus has.

Even the simple act of eating has been plundered by New Ageism, which would have us believe that we can evolve into higher spiritual states through what we eat or through herbal medicines that we ingest. Many people are unwittingly being seduced by the health food craze as Satan attempts to lure health food fanatics to be "god" in their own lives. Obviously eating wisely is physically beneficial, but to suggest it has spiritual merit, too, is a Pagan concept.

A warning light should flash when *anything* apart from the power of Jesus Christ claims to have the ability to "heal the whole"—body, mind and spirit.

Digging up the Past

Another technique growing in mainstream acceptance and supposedly designed to restore wholeness and health is the art of regression. This meditative therapy, borrowed from pagan rituals, uses the power of the imagination to regress the patient back into the womb or even further back into past lives. Past-life regression is closely linked to the cruel belief in reincarnation. As lying spirits play spiritual mind-games, the bait is set for occultic intrusion.

Non-Christian therapies have their counterparts in the Christian community too. For example, "inner healing" or "emotional spiritual healing" in the church uses the so-called "wisdom" (occult psychic powers) of ancient religious techniques. These are disguised in an assortment of self-help therapies which rely on hypnosis, mental relaxation, yoga, meditation, and visualization. However, God will not be manipulated by us, no matter how we attempt to walk Him through the corridors of our minds and direct Him to heal our emotions. God performs miracles outside of us through His sovereign intervention. He does not respond to our exploitation. Unfortunately, many Christians are being seduced by these techniques, which use human psychic powers and conjure up spirits for assistance. The Bible explicitly forbids such practices.

In principle the idea of spiritual wholeness is a biblical one. But, once again, the sly handiwork of Satan the counterfeiter is seen in the arts of New Age shamanism. Assuming that "the Force" is the healing power instead of "the Source of the force" is the seductive lie that traps believers as well as unbelievers.

The Deceptive Promise of Godhood

The basic idea of man progressing from simple to complex, from mortality to godhood, is the underlying notion in New Age thinking. Richard Greene, founder of the Mind Control Institute, sums this up in an interview for the film *The Evolution Conspiracy* when he says:

> What's going on with this New Age is that we've been making a transition in different levels

of evolution. Evolution is going on all the time. Many people believe, as I do, that the purpose of life is to grow and that you grow as much as you can in each lifetime, and of course we believe in reincarnation. We have mastered the evolution of the body now; that happened thousands of millions of years ago. That has remained relatively static. We have now moved into the period of our evolution as humankind where we are evolving mentally...

The hundredth monkey phenomenon states that when a certain level of humanity reaches a certain level of consciousness that it's going to catch on like wildfire. Very similar to Buckminster Fuller's theory for critical mass, when there's a certain amount of energy, it takes quantum leaps.

I believe that if every human opens up to the possibility of there being a spiritual dimension that we will evolve individually and that will lead into the evolution of the species. Our purpose on earth is to make ourselves realize our godhood, that we have everything that we need inside of us... We're in a time now where man is literally taking control of his own evolution.

The delusion that man is "literally taking control of his own evolution" is ludicrous in light of events that are reported daily. To imagine that we can draw from resources within ourselves as we "realize our godhood" is clear deception. The Bible says that "the heart is deceitful above all things, and desperately wicked" (Jeremiah 17:9). Solutions of goodness cannot come from man's imagining that his heart is evolving to a higher state of purity, but only from God who can put a clean heart inside of man: "Create in me a clean heart, O God; and renew a right spirit within me" (Psalm 51:10).

Humanism based on a foundation that rejects God is gaining spiritual momentum among millions today who believe that within man is the potential of "God power." A new generation is turning back to paganism rooted in evolutionism, which promotes this religious theory.

John Randolph Price in his book *The Superbeings* says:

> A new species of man is coming forth to lead us out of darkness and into a new dimension scarcely dreamed of by ninety percent of this world. This will be the New Age of Enlightenment, and science and religion will join hands in spreading the truth that man is not the man we thought he was. I thank God that I live at this time and will be able to see the next great leap forward in man's expanding consciousness."[3]

This "superconsciousness" is renamed "god consciousness within," "the god-power," "the christ-within." These are just some of the names given to man's prideful claim that he is God, and can do what only God is able to do. This spiritual mirage leads millions to what they think is soul-satisfying water. But as with any mirage, it is only an illusion.

If the New Ager chooses to imagine that he has the ability to control his immortality, Satan will impress upon him the means with which to do it. If the would-be reincarnationist wants to believe that he has the ability to come back in another life, Satan will find a form of deception that will cause him to believe it. The same principle applies to the evolutionist who has been duped into believing that he came from nothing and goes to nothing. Satan is like a chameleon and can change his color to suit the need of the moment.

The apostle Peter understood this. His warning is clear: "Be on the alert. Your adversary, the devil, prowls about like a roaring lion, seeking someone to devour" (1 Peter 5:8 NASB).

Jesus also spoke of the reality of the devil and his deadly plot, "The thief comes only to steal, and kill, and destroy; I came that they might have life, and might have it abundantly" (John 10:10 NASB).

There are millions today who have chosen to reject God the Creator's grace through Jesus Christ. Countless others have not yet been presented with the choice. Thousands upon thousands are turning away from the traditional Judeo-Christian faith of their parents or grandparents and choosing paganism instead. Disillusioned by materialism, churchism, secularism, and humanism, seekers of self-fulfillment are turning to this new evolutionary religiosity and embracing the lie that they can become gods, or at least have the power to control their lives and destiny. Assured of inward resources and psychic powers, they attempt to substitute these for the God-convicting vacuum inside.

Every Man a God

The concept that man can evolve into higher states or godhood is fraudulent, scandalous, and a complete sham that should motivate Christians with a burning desire to fight the good fight. As Martin Luther said:

> If I profess with the loudest voice and clearest expression every portion of the truth of God

except precisely that little point which the world and the devil are at that moment attacking, I am not confessing Christ, however boldly I may be professing Christ. Where the battle rages, there the loyalty of the soldier is proved, and to be steady on all the battlefield besides, is mere flight and disgrace if he flinches at that point."

The New Age promise of spiritual control is the same lie perpetrated by Satan when he seduced Eve in the garden of Eden (Genesis.3:4,5). It was the same spirit of rebellion that resulted in Satan being cast out of the presence of God. Isaiah 14 recounts Satan's story from God's perspective. Lucifer, the "day-star," with all his God-given beauty and authority, brought rebellion into the universe when in his heart he said "I will" and set his mind on things outside of God.

Today this rebellion continues. Well-known pagan evangelist and actress Shirley MacLaine, in the popular television mini-series "Out on a Limb," stood on Malibu Beach in Southern California, her arms extended. She repeated over and over again: "I am God, I am God, I am God...." Millions were watching when this prime-time show aired.

This sort of self-deification is disturbing enough in the secular world, but consider what some Christian televangelists are saying:

Morris Cerillo says, "We are made in the image of God, a small miniature God...act like a God."[4]

Benny Hinn says, "Within me is a God-man...I am a God-man...you are a little god running around."[5]

Kenneth Copeland says, "We are partakers of the divine nature...you don't have a God in you, you are one!"[6] "Adam is as much like a god as you could get, just the same as Jesus...he's God manifested in the flesh..."[7] "I say this and repeat it so it doesn't upset you too bad . . . when I read in the Bible where He [Jesus] says, 'I Am,' I say, 'Yes! I am too!' "[8]

Earl Paulk says, "Until we comprehend that we are little gods and we begin to act like little gods, we cannot manifest the kingdom of God."[9]

Kenneth Copeland's most startling statement fits into the New Age movement's agenda all too well: "Jesus was the firstborn man to ever be born from sin to righteousness. He was the pattern of a new race of men to come."[10]

Satan's deception, that man can become God, is now being taken dangerously further. As he schemed to build a unified government with spiritual aspirations in Babel, so again today he is attempting to manipulate mass consciousness. He is convincing mankind that global unity and man-made "peace" will ultimately overcome God's revealed Word about the coming end of the planet.

Evolution and Mother Earth

A planet-attentive political perspective with its emphasis on global ecological cooperation and religious tolerance is capturing countless souls as they seek world cooperation in bringing about this false peace on planet Earth.

Biblical Christianity, Orthodox Judaism, and the Muslim faith are the only religions based on creation. All other religions are based on evolution. They fundamentally agree that chaotic forces and processes of nature, sometimes personified as gods and goddesses, birthed the present situation.

In India, chaos, mayhem, and destruction are worshiped as the creative force in the form of the goddess Kali. She is seen as the looming menace behind nature and as the ruler over all the dark elements of nature. In her evolutionary role she is seen as "the cruel, unpitying, avenging side of the cosmic process."[11]

Kali was represented in several old religions—she was Isis in Ancient Egypt, Black Venus in Rome, Black Demeter in Ancient Greece. Her other names are Great Mother, Mother Nature, and Mother Earth. Her modern name in our Western culture is Gaia, and a Gaia hypothesis has evolved over the last 20 years as a European spiritual sister to evolution. It has its own branch of science ceremoniously called geophysiology, the science of planetary medicine.

Its originator, Dr. James Lovelock, sees our planet's system of life and environment as spiritually and inextricably coupled. He says that the two aspects, rather like two sides of the same coin, have co-evolved and cooperated in a mutually interchangeable role for billions of years.

At its end-of-the-decade review, the British newspaper, *The Times*, credited the Gaian hypothesis "as perhaps the most significant movement in thought in the 1980's."[12] By April 1990 this big new idea culminated in the largest worldwide demonstration in history ... "Earthday" a festival acknowledging Gaia, or Mother Earth, as a spirit-life who is believed to have nurtured all life-forms and environment since the dawn of time.

Gaians, the new neopagans, see themselves as those who have been "awakened" by the new spiritual, global consciousness. They speculate that if we "citizens of the earth" don't treat "our Mother Earth" with respect, then Mother Goddess Gaia will turn on us just as a human body takes action against a dangerous virus. That is why it is necessary to lay aside long-held religious and political animosities to care for Mother Earth. In this religious concept the earth has not only been personified but deified too. Gaia's spiritual purpose is to raise global consciousness and introduce planetary "science," which presupposes that people are intimately connected to each other and to every species of animal and every lump of rock on the planet. This generation's mission, in the Gaian agenda, is to "heal the planet" as though she were a sick person.

Everyone knows that good stewardship of our planet is a legitimate concern. However, the Gaian global political agenda is much more ominous than an awareness of simple ecology might imply. The new global peace movement seeks to bring about Planet Management, which examines the relationship between militarization and global ecology and proposes New Age paths to peace. Peace is seen as "personal harmony and harmony in man's relationship with the totality of all life, [and] the best way ... is said to be through co-operation not conflict."[13]

Even children are being swept into Gaian theology. Witness Ted Turner's Saturday-morning cartoon program, "Captain Planet." Turner, who once said that Christianity was "for losers," preaches ecology and goddess worship on the show. "The Power is yours" is the message of this series.

Despite man's wishes, a global peace built by man and based on evolution will not result in the spiritual wholeness that people are bartering their eternal destinies for. Rather it paves the way for a new world order—and Satan's last hope to destroy man's relationship with his Creator.

Satan's Final Strategy

There is a school of thought gaining acceptability which states that when the collective consciousness of the "spiritually attuned masses" attains a certain level of awareness there will be a quantum leap into *global spiritual oneness*.

This will form a spiritual basis for the coming new world order. People will believe that their combined efforts of consciousness make the quantum leap into peace possible. This outlook plays right into the hands of Satan, who has one final strategy left in his battle for men's souls.

The Bible tells us that at the appointed time Jesus the Messiah, will return as the King of Kings, to rule as the Prince of Peace for a thousand years. He will also bring down a new earth from heaven, one that will be totally free from Satan's interference.

Obviously the passionate jealousy of Satan is attempting to overthrow such inevitable plans, plans which include eternal destruction for Satan and those who choose to follow him. In his last ploy, Satan will lure men away from allegiance to their Creator. He will satisfy men with a false peace and ultimately usher in a false world leader, whom the Bible calls the Antichrist. This man will deceive millions as they perceive him to be the global leadership they have all looked forward to. With accelerating speed we see mankind being conditioned to just such a scenario. Today's media reports extensively detail the trends of global political unity, man's hope of a new world order, and discussions of global financial economy. We see mainline Christian denominations moving toward religious ecumenism that embraces not only liberal religious ideas but also pagan philosophies and religions which hold evolution dear.

Profoundly revolutionary are the new missionary goals of this blossoming movement. It vehemently challenges age-old values and morals which are rooted in the Bible. Old ways of thinking, no matter how cherished and useful in the past, have no place within modern man's massive religio-political trend.

Jeremy Rifkin, leading New Age spokesperson, says:

We no longer feel ourselves to be guests in someone else's home and therefore obliged to make our behavior conform with a set of pre-existing cosmic rules. It is our creation now. We make the rules. We establish the parameters of reality. We create the world, and because we do, we no longer feel beholden to outside forces. We no longer have to justify our behavior, for we are now the architects of the universe. We are responsible to nothing outside ourselves, for we are the kingdom, the power, and the glory forever and ever.[14]

The Kingdom, Here and Now

The idea that man can build his own kingdom of heaven on earth distorts the Christian's biblical hope of the true heaven and breeds horrendous apostasy in the church. This condition is prophesied in 2 Thessalonians 2:3, which says that before the Antichrist, or false messiah, can assert himself as world leader of Satan's kingdom on earth, there is to be a "falling away" from the church. Millions of so-called Christians have become corrupted by the world's agenda, and are even now playing into the hands of the enemy in his quest to dupe men into believing that world consolidation will bring about a satisfying peace.

The Reconstructionists, a growing movement significantly affecting the evangelical church, claim that Christ's return is dependent upon a global political takeover by *Christians* who must establish His kingdom on earth before He can return. Advocates of Kingdom and Dominion Theology join in the dangerous perpetration of such heresy. Certain charismatics in mainline denominations and some Catholic Renewal movements fall into the same apostasy, adopting Latter Rain and Manifest Sons of God theology which claim that a "raising" of Christian consciousness is necessary to restore God's earthly kingdom.

"Christianity is destined to take over all the kingdoms of the earth" says David Chilton.[15]

"God wants Christians to control the earth on His behalf... (We) want to see a Biblical reconstruction of the United States, so that it can serve as an example to be followed all over the world," says reconstructionist Gary North.[16]

How presumptuous to think that God needs the help of either Christians or nonbelievers to accomplish His destiny! The Christian's citizenship is not here on earth but in heaven (1 Peter 1:17). To conquer the world for God is not the ministry to which God called His church. To compromise the Great Commission is to do a corrupt disservice to the command of Christ.

Jesus said, "Go ye therefore, and teach all nations, baptizing them in the name of the Father, and of the Son, and of the Holy Ghost, teaching them to observe all things whatsoever I have commanded you" (Matthew 28:19,20).

Among other important truths Jesus taught creationism, and that may be the best place to start in evangelizing nonbelievers today!

Unfortunately, the Reconstructionists are not the only religious group playing a part in the move toward manmade world peace. Sadly, some Roman Catholic leaders including the pope are being used as catalysts to usher in ecumenicalism and political "harmony" on earth. Ultimately this calls for submission to a leader whom all will mistakenly believe to be the "Prince of Peace" and the Messiah. This completely redirects the hope of millions of people from the Rapture (the event spoken of in 1 Thessalonians 4:16,17 when believers in Jesus are removed from the earth) to an unsatisfactory plan of heaven on earth under the authority of a false leader. (For further reading on the "Christianizing" of planet Earth read *Whatever Happened to Heaven* by Dave Hunt.)

The Reconstructionists will see this world leader as the "Christ" that they were able to usher in due to their important political maneuvering.

Liberals within the Catholic Church and other political Christian groups will praise him as a genius of global political peace, as will millions of others worldwide.

The Jews will gratefully acclaim him as the peacemaker, their long-awaited "Messiah."

The evolutionists will see him as naturalistic emanation that formed from the cosmic universe, which at last scientifically proves that order can come out of chaos.

The Infinite Wisdom of God

As we analyze our society, it is easy to see that we are being steeped in the concept that physical evolution is responsible for shaping the past and that spiritual evolution is able to create our future.

To accept the outrageous idea that godhood lies within man, not only as a personal evolutionary pilgrimage but on a grand scale, brings heavy warnings from God: "Because your heart is lifted up and you have said, 'I am a god, I sit in the seat of gods, I sit in the midst of the seas'; yet you are a man, and not God, although you make your heart like the heart of God ... behold, I will bring strangers upon you, the most ruthless of the nations. And they shall draw their swords against the beauty of your wisdom, and defile your splendor" (Ezekiel 28:2,7 NASB).

History has proved that man's godhood can never happen. Anytime that man attempts to rule the universe, he must fall. To believe that man can bring in an age of lasting peace apart from God is to believe the lie that out of chaos comes order. But method cannot come out of madness.

Method and order are the faithful characteristics of a God of love, and are transparently seen in His creation. Method and order belong to a God with eternal intentions, who gracefully shows that every jot and tittle in the Bible have an ultimate purpose in revealing Him as Truth and Love. Method and order are part of the infinite wisdom of a God filled with the purpose of bringing mankind into a loving relationship with Him, a God who died for the love of His enemies, who gave His life for truth.

CHAPTER 11

Eternity in the Wings

There will come a day when every bug, worm, burrowing rabbit, rat, and wombat under the earth will give praise to the Creator God. Every tiny and large bird of the skies. Every variety of animal from the African desert to the tropical rain forest. Every crab and sandpiper, freshwater fish, deep-sea fish, and sea-monster. Even the clam will no longer be clammed up! The apostle Paul notes that creation will be released from its slavery to corruption into freedom (Romans 8:21). All creation will raise its voice in perfect harmony to give praise to God and His Son Jesus, the precious Lamb, God's unblemished sacrifice.

The apostle John tells us of this future event in his revelation: "And every creature which is in heaven, and on the earth, and under the earth, and such as are in the sea, and all that are in them, heard I saying, Blessing, and honor, and glory, and power, be unto him that sits upon the throne, and unto the Lamb for ever and ever" (Revelation 5:13).

Even now there is a resounding chorus of continual praise and worship offered to God for His creation by His heavenly hosts, the angels. John continues: "And I beheld, and I heard the voice of many angels... the number of them was ten thousand times ten thousand, and thousands of thousands; saying with a loud voice, Worthy is the Lamb that was slain to receive power, and riches, and wisdom, and strength, and honor, and glory, and blessing" (Revelation 5:11,12).

As if the mind-boggling harmony of such synchronization isn't enough to overwhelm our human senses, there is the added concord of those "who rest not day and night, saying, Holy, holy, holy, Lord God Almighty, which was, and is, and is to come" (Revelation 4:8). And still another section of the heavenlies add, "Thou are worthy, O Lord, to receive glory and honor and power: for Thou hast created all things, and for Thy pleasure they are and were created" (Revelation 4:11)!

While many people reject creation and opt for belief in evolution, God's heavenly host are reflecting on His glorious acts of creation, declaring Him worthy of glory and honor and praise and confirming that all He has accomplished is to His glory and for our benefit. Can we on earth even imagine the love God has for us despite mankind's rejection of Him? Those who believe in creation should stand in awe at the power of God who continues to sustain the existence of earth solely by His Word and loving purpose.

The book of Hebrews tells us that God's Son not only made the world but "upholds all things by the word of His power" (Hebrews 1:3 NASB. Many people wonder why He continues to do this. The Bible answers, "The Lord is not slow about His promise, as some count slowness, but is patient toward you, not wishing for any to perish but for all to come to repentance" (2 Peter 3:9 NASB).

God wants everyone to be drawn to the truth that Jesus Christ is His Son, His Salvation, and His promised Messiah. According to God's will, the day will come when Jesus will gather His faithful believers to Himself (2 Thessalonians 2:1) and later descend to reveal Himself as the ruler of God's kingdom, a kingdom in which righteousness will dwell. This will be a new heaven and earth; the old one will be destroyed with fire (2 Peter 3:10-13)

Unconquerable God

As we have looked at many facets of the evolution conspiracy, we have seen that our culture is slamming the door on God the Creator, while at the same time opening the door to the *fallen* spiritual realm (the demonic realm). As a result, people are increasingly embracing Satan's false promise that they are the masters of their own world.

This lie has become more firmly entrenched as the evolution conspiracy has tried in every way possible to remove God from His rightful position as Creator. As we have seen, it has done this in science, in education, and in popular culture by undermining faith in God's revealed Word, the Bible. Tampering with the authority and intent of God's written Word has serious consequences which God severely warns about (see Revelation 21:19). The Bible teaches that man was created by God, fell from God's grace as a result of disobedience and is desperately in need of redemption. This truth has been a stumbling block to many who choose rather to believe that man was not created by God, but evolved and is the end product of some unguided process of chance and time. Man's pride argues that the biblical perspective of creation is unscientific, without admitting to the unreasonable assumption of evolutionism.

Evolutionism's attempts to rid man of knowledge and trust in the biblical God of creation cannot curb humankind's incurable desire for supernatural fellowship and worship. Man was created to worship, and whether he worships the Creator God, or other idols including himself, his spiritual drive must be met. In response to such needs, evolutionary thinking has embraced many humanist and New Age concepts. This is nothing short of Satan's lie to Eve in Genesis 3:4,5: "You will not die; you will be like God."

By accepting the idea of "godhood" (that man is in control of his own power and destiny), modern man buys into the very same hoax that seduced Eve in the first place. The power that was promised her was a counterfeit offered by the one who wanted to draw her away from her dependence on and relationship with God.

Millions of people are being duped by the false spiritual idea that our society continues on an upward evolutionary pathway upward, that mankind is on the verge of entering a brand-new age of consciousness and awareness that will come as a so-called quantum leap in man's evolutionary process. As we are presently witnessing in today's society, man's decision to eliminate God by propagating the lie of evolution has ignited a wildfire of New Age thinking and mentality which openly encourages contact with the occult, worship of self, and denial of a biblical God.

The primary way that mankind establishes a powerful relationship with the true biblical God is through careful meditation in His Word, the Bible. "The word of God is living and active and sharper than any two-edged sword, and piercing as far as the division of soul and spirit, of both joints and marrow, and able to judge the thoughts and intentions of the heart" (Hebrews 4:12 NASB). The Bible, this mighty sword of the Christian warrior, is increasingly and deliberately being undermined in schools and even churches, many of which dismiss its content as symbolic and irrelevant.

An example of blatant misrepresentation was witnessed at the recent Jesus Seminar. The Jesus Seminar is a a 200-member group of Bible scholars including teachers from universities and seminaries and even representatives of the Society of Biblical Literature. This group, which began in 1985, has ruled out the authenticity of 80 percent of the words attributed to Jesus from the Gospels. It has concluded that the Lord's Prayer does not go back to the historical Jesus. It has rejected such important Christian foundations as John 3:16 and John 14:6 ("I am the way, the truth, and the life; no man comes to the Father, but by me.") These people have systematically attempted to invalidate the Messiah's sacrifice of His blood for the atonement of man's sins. They have also assaulted His unique character as God and the teaching of His inevitable return to rule on earth. But the unbeliever's skeptical view of God and of the faithful authority of His Word cannot change God's eternal purpose. God is not mocked.

Ultimately, Satan cannot and will not win in his conspiracy against God, but is doomed to a thousand years in chains, imprisoned in the bottomless pit. After that he will eventually be cast into the lake of fire burning with brimstone (Revelation 20). At times however, many people question God's ways and purposes and Satan is credited with winning the battle. At the crucifixion of Jesus, all the "rulers, powers, the world forces of darkness and spiritual forces of wickedness in the heavenly places (Ephesians 6:12) must have believed that they had successfully killed the "King of the Jews" and thwarted His eternal plan. For three days Satan's accomplices were filled with arrogant pride at their accomplishment. But then unconquerable

God overpowered death and presented Himself resurrected to His triumphant followers. His resurrection represented the future hope of all believers, the hope of eternity in His presence.

A Love Story

She was young and pure, and very beautiful. But more impressive than her physical appearance was her inner loveliness. Her heart had been transformed by the love of her fiance. Her devotion to this young man and their plans for the future, which they had discussed so intimately before he left her, was her strength.

Indeed the assurance of his faithful love letters satisfied her hope and encouraged her through the passing years. In reading his letters repeatedly she would often discover a new aspect of him that she had somehow missed before. As her love grew deeper, so did her trust for him. He'd vowed that, upon his return he would wipe away her tears and there would only be joy. With such deep hope and confidence, she went about her daily tasks meditating on the one she loved.

Her joy would rise to soaring heights if friends or family asked for news of her betrothed's latest adventures. At such precious moments she would share his letters.

Uncle Earnest was an archaeologist and particularly interested in the aspects of the fiance's letters that dealt with ancient peoples and cities. Wanting to be careful of her feelings, he nevertheless felt it his duty to carefully point out historical inconsistencies in his reporting. Unable to combat the authenticity of each historical detail, she conceded that her fiance's reporting might be flawed.

Earnest's wife was an anthropologist. She took issue with the parts of the letters that spoke on the customs and behaviors of the primitive people. She described them as barbarians and paraphrased the words of Charles Darwin, "Why, one can hardly make oneself believe that they are fellow creatures; your fiance's love and sacrifice for them seem quite inappropriate."

Condescendingly, the young woman's aunt patted her on the back of her hand. She triumphantly noticed her niece's confidence shake further as she attacked the motives of her intended. The girl grieved for her suitor. As she inwardly resigned herself to his lack of scientific knowledge, she mourned over his wasted compassion and fruitless mission to those far-off peoples.

Grandfather George was a meteorologist, and gulped on his evening sherry with noticeable aggravation as he considered the letters' mention of atmospheric phenomena, signs of weather and various climate conditions. Why, they were contrary to scientific explanation! Fully aware of his granddaughter's keen affection for the young man, he stooped to offer consolation and attempted to reassure the young woman that the field was full of complexities far beyond a layman's comprehension. With regrets, she sighed as she submitted herself to the innocence and simplicity of her betrothed.

Bespectacled, stern, and officious was Mr. Allison-Wadley, a friend of the family and headmaster of the neighboring Learning Academy. By reputation he was considered the leading expert in handwriting, a paleographer.

He argued that the letters did not reflect the penmanship of the true author by comparison to previously written material from his school days. The spelling form, alphabetization, and ideographics were contradictory, and it was obvious to him that a collaborator had coauthored or solely composed the contents. In consideration of profuse academic and scholarly proof generously offered by the

famous Allison-Wadley, the gracious young woman conceded that perhaps that was the case.

Her cheerful disposition waned over the months as she
slowly accepted the systematic criticism of her letters. Her
joy and love had been slowly diffused, draining the strength
from her soul. The heaviness of her heart made her unable
to bear the burdens of daily life. She wept over her lost
love, questioned her own naive trust in him, and sought
gratification elsewhere. But nothing else could fill her
vacuum of love. Empty desperation drove her back to
search the once-precious love letters to find any shred of
truth that had not been destroyed.

Her dear governess attempted to comfort her.

"My dear one, in all his numerous letters to you he didn't
clearly mention when he would return again; perhaps he
is unable to return. Perhaps he won't be back at all. He
has, after all, been away so many years." She paused.
"Perhaps he never really cared for you, dear. How could he
have loved you if he left you?"

Tears of desperation filled the girl's eyes. The only
remaining thread of frayed hope was being snapped in two.

Then, from somewhere deep within her heart, an undeniable truth began to stir.

No one ever knew her lover's heart as she did. He had
always been as good as his word in the past. His word was
truth then. Why wouldn't it be so now and in the future?
Somehow in that spirit of trust and with confidence in the
authority of his words she knew that he loved her and
would come back for her.

Her heart began to feel strengthened. How could she
have allowed his critics to influence her? They had based
their view of his character only on their own limited experience and on hearsay. She had allowed them to weaken
her love for him without a shred of hard evidence. Her

beloved's experience had certainly gone far beyond what they could understand. When he returned, he would explain every detail of his letters to their complete understanding. With reawakened enthusiasm, she once again claimed his love letters as true. They were written by him alone, for her alone. Those letters were her reassurance of his undeniable love for her and their destiny together.

The hope of his return rushed back like life-blood into her veins. She found purpose again. His love had never changed—she had only fallen away in her heart. And when the day arrived, the day he would return at last, she would be ready. She was waiting for him.

Our Beloved Bridegroom

Jesus likened Himself to a bridegroom who, in the Jewish tradition of the day, would snatch up his faithful bride and carry her to the house that he had built onto his father's home. The bride then spent seven intimate days alone with the groom. At the end of this time the groom would present his bride to all of the other guests and the marriage supper would proceed. Paul too compares the believer's intimate relationship with Jesus to marriage (Ephesians 5:32). And Revelation says that Jesus will present His bride to the rest of the world, "for the marriage of the Lamb has come and His bride has made herself ready.... Blessed are those who are invited to the marriage supper of the Lamb" (Revelation 19:7,9 NASB).

Jesus will one day gather His bride, just as He promised. Bible prophecy also predicts a seven-year period of devastating tribulation for those left on earth who are deceived into believing in the power of an imposter who will set himself up above all, "the son of destruction, who opposes and exalts himself above every so-called god or object of worship, so that he takes his seat in the temple of God, displaying himself as being God" (2 Thessalonians 2:4 NASB).

This false messiah will offer a deceptive sense of peace that will appear to be the new world order that mankind has longed for ever since the fall of Adam and Eve. It will be a counterfeit attempt at God's promised new heaven and earth, and new Holy City Jerusalem.

The period of false peace will end with the second coming of Jesus Christ, the true Messiah. The apostle John pictures this momentous event for us: "Behold, he comes with clouds: and every eye shall see him, and they also which pierced him: and all kindreds of the earth shall wail because of Him" (Revelation 1:7).

At this second coming even the unbelievers will see Jesus for who He is. Many evolutionists will be pressed to gaze down the evolutionary ladder in remorse. They will wail and lament their defeat and His victory over them, but their pride will persist, and no remorse or repentance of heart will be able to change them. They are doomed to torture and separation from God for all eternity.

When all is finished, the famous Isaiah passage that is printed on millions of Christmas cards every year will finally come to pass: "For unto us a child is born, unto us a son is given: and the government shall be upon his shoulder: and his name shall be called Wonderful, Counselor, The mighty God, The everlasting Father, The Prince of Peace" (Isaiah 9:6).

The happy union of Christ with his bride, the faithful, will continue to be joyously celebrated as the real and truly peaceful New World Order, reigned over by Jesus Christ Himself in the New Jerusalem, is ushered in. This is the hope of the church, the secure and joyful destiny of every person who confesses that Jesus Christ is Lord.

In the end, all will see that God has been true to His truthful Word. When Christ returns, He will give those who have held to His truth the reward of their faithfulness. They will delight in worshiping Him forever in His presence.

Despite Satan's plans, plans which include the evolution conspiracy, God continues to attempt to lovingly lead people into personal fellowship with Himself. God's timing is perfect. He has a purpose in everything. And until He returns, those who belong to Him must fervently seek to rescue people from an eternity apart from God. We must deny evolutionary fables that dull man's thirst for true spiritual satisfaction. And we must lovingly introduce people to the One who, with His blood, purchased eternal life for all those who would believe.

> In the beginning was the Word, and the Word was with God, and the Word was God. He was in the beginning with God. All things came into being by Him; and apart from Him nothing came into being that has come into being. In Him was life, and the life was the light of men. And the light shines in the darkness, and the darkness did not comprehend it (John 1:1-5 NASB).

Appendicies

Notes

Recommended Reading

National Creationist
Organizations

Foreign Creationist
Organizations

The Grand Canyon's Mysteries

Like an erratic dragonfly, our small "glass bubble" hummed over vast tree-tops. We fidgeted nervously, trying to get used to the new sensation of our first helicopter journey. We watched the helicopter's distorted shadow as it playfully skipped over the pine forest, less than a hundred feet below us. Earphones pressed to our heads played out a raspy rendition of the *2001 Space Odyssey* soundtrack.

Without warning the ground fell several thousand feet below us as we passed over the edge of the magnificent Grand Canyon. We all grasped at our safety belts and gasped deeply. Inside our glass machine we had the illusion of being a vacuum within a vacuum. There was nothing substantial between us and all of nature around us, and it appeared as though we were hanging in void. It was both terrifying and awesome. The wind caught our blades and held us motionless for what seemed like too long. We were numbed by the discovery of our frail vulnerability. We became conscious of our smallness and insignificance as we hung suspended inside the earth's vast chasm. Over 2,000 square miles of scenic wonderland sprawled all around us. Size lost all proportion. Time and space were deprived of any relevance in this uncanny, mammoth surrounding.

The immense expanse of enormous mountain ranges, rock formations, and breathtaking beauty gave a fantasy-like quality to the entire experience. We seemed hung like fragile puppets in an environment that forcibly witnessed the presence of a powerful authority. We were overwhelmed by the astonishing proportions of this monstrous ravine.

There is no question that the very soul of man is provoked into a spiritual worship when gazing at the cathedral-like sculptures of the majestic rocks. The stained-glass colors reflecting in the mighty Colorado River. The almost angelic choir of sounds splashing from the vivacious rapids and dancing waterfalls. The cloistered peace of the tropical rain forest. All these are set amidst the reverent backdrop of the Grand Canyon.

Obviously the early explorers who named the precipitous bluffs and towering buttes felt moved by the mystical power of the Grand Canyon. It is understandable that some mountains reflect the names of explorers who discovered them and events and names of Arizona pioneers. It is also commendable that acknowledgment is given to the five Native American Indian tribes who still live in the region. However, it almost seems an intentional oversight that no reminder, no indication of praise, and no implication of glory, is given to the creative power of the God of Jews and Christians. It is equally hard to understand why more than half of the names used to identify the rock formations were drawn from pagan gods, their philosophies, and from ghoulish concepts.

In Search of a New World

The majority of America's founders were driven to

establish America by the inspiration of their belief in a sovereign God. It is interesting to note, however, that many of them were influenced by Freemasonry. Freemasonry, which clearly contradicts Christianity, was a visible political influence. The power it wields is evidenced by some of its occult symbolism, seen in the Great Seal of the United States—its pyramid and "third eye" depicted on the one-dollar bill. It is also represented by the use of the now-familiar phrase, "A New World Order" (Novus Ordo Seclorum), printed under the pyramid, a phrase which promotes the most important goal of all Freemasons.

Freemasonry's inspiration is not surprisingly noted in the Grand Canyon. The main explorations to this magnificent national park began in 1854. Major John Wesley Powell, a one-armed Civil War veteran, and members of his various expeditions are credited for the naming of much of the Canyon in 1871 to 1902. Members of the original Grand Canyon Masonic Lodge confirm "that it would be logical to presume that Powell was a Mason, because many at that time were, and names pertaining to the craft are all around the Grand Canyon."[1]

The Grand Canyon's pagan heritage is a sad reflection of spiritual compromise which influences millions of tourists annually. Instead of taking the opportunity to inspire mankind to acknowledge God through His creation, the Grand Canyon has become an education in world mysticism and an introduction to ancient nature beliefs, paganism, and myths that the Bible refers to as Babylonian idolatry.

The Meaning of Grand Canyon's Names

Scanning any Grand Canyon map, one may be surprised

to notice the conglomeration of philosophies and myth-
ological deities represented. Despite possible contradic-
tions within their teachings, the philosophies represented
in the canyon share the common thread that evolution
resulted in the world's birth, and is the beginning of all
life.

The Hindu triad is prominently featured on the east side
of the Grand Canyon near the "Hindu Amphitheater."
Shiva, Brahma, and Vishnu, according to India's bible, the
Gita, are said to have shared in creation with the activities
of Brahman. Brahman is supposed to be the supreme
energy of neutral and impersonal origin, the cause and
basis of all existence.

The seventh and eighth incarnations (consecutively) of
Vishnu are said to be Rama and Krishna. Both these
Hindu deities have been given their own "shrines" near
their soul-forefather's memorial, Vishnu Temple. The
interchangeable ideas of evolution and reincarnation are
reflected in the blasphemous counterfeit of the Biblical
trinity reflected in the Hindu triad: Brahma—the power
to create; Vishnu, the power to preserve; and Shiva—the
power to destroy.

Buddha Temple, situated in Bright Angel Canyon in the
center of Grand Canyon, gives tribute to Gautama (Buddha), who taught the theology of evolution. He was born in
563 B.C., and was the Indian sage who founded Buddhism.
Buddha is a title meaning "enlightened one." In Gautama's
theology this meant one who had acquired salvation by
mystically cutting himself off from the surrounding reality of life. Gautama saw lust for power, success, money, sex,
and bodily comforts as the root of all unhappiness, and
he contended that all such passions should be overcome
through self-deprivation. Unlike Christian benevolence,
which urges its followers to love others and practice social

justice, Buddhism requires that such passionate zeal be dismissed along with the desires for self-gratification. Both motivations are seen to be similarly undesirable.

Reverenced in Freemasonry along with other "reformers" of *equal* standing are Zoroaster, Jesus, and Confucius. The latter's philosophy gave rise to the martial art known as Kung Fu. "Kung" was Confucius' family name and "Fu" literally means "scholar." A Grand Canyon rock, known as Confucius Temple, is named in his honor.

Chinese religion is based in concepts of evolutionism and reincarnation and is often mistakenly understood in the West as merely a philosophy, distinct from religion. John Berthrong explains: "Confucianism, especially, became a religion without any great speculation on the nature and function of God. For this reason it was often not even considered to be a religion. However, it is clear that Confucianism is a religion and that it was the dominant tradition of pre-modern China. . . . There is a persistent belief in the balance of nature, an idea which was later explicitly defined as the famous concepts of Yin and Yang, the forces of dark and light, soft and hard, of female and male."[2]

Zoroaster of Persia was a contemporary of Confucius and in his honor one of the highest elevations in the Grand Canyon has been named Zoroaster Temple. Although separated by much of Asia, Zoroaster and Confucius were part of a great freedom movement dedicated to release the human mind from allegiance to a corrupt priesthood and existing polytheism. Gautama's Buddhism came out of this movement too, when "Buddha," who was probably an atheist, revolted against the existing priesthood of the day, its priest-craft, and the caste system.

Zoroaster, a priest and prophet, taught that God, who only created that which is good, created man as His representative. "[God] created a number of heavenly beings... the Bounteous Immortals... the sons and daughters of God, as they became known.... There is an important abstract dimension to their nature, as their names show... Mind... Righteousness... Devotion... Wholeness... Immortality... [these] are ideals to which the righteous should aspire. So by sharing in the good mind, by a life of devotion and righteousness, man shares in God's dominion and attains wholeness and immortality...."[3] One can see that Zoroaster's thinking parallels much of today's humanism.

In the Grand Canyon the dragon has been edified with its own gulch, The Dragon, south of which lies Dragon Head. In the Bible the dragon is defined as "that ancient serpent, who is the devil, or Satan," also known as the one who deceives the nations (Revelation 20:2). Throughout the Bible he is associated with corruption, evil, and sin. However all other cultures see the serpent as a symbol of spiritual well-being, feminism, reincarnation, and evolutionism.

Fred Gettings, in his *Dictionary of Demons*, writes, "In occult and esoteric symbolism the dragon is more often than not a symbol of initiation. The dragon is either a creature of air or a creature of water who lives upon the earth, and thus becomes an apt symbol for an initiate who, through the fact of his initiation, has the ability to live in two worlds (on the earth and on the spiritual plane) at the same time."

Evolutionism is honored on the eastern side of the Grand Canyon by a host of Roman and Greek gods and goddesses. The beliefs and philosophies of these skeptics, epicureans, stoics, and cynics are similar to many of today's pagan strains of thinking.

The Greeks had a precise understanding of their gods, while the Romans had not defined theirs clearly. When the Romans conquered Greece they merged their myths, integrated their philosophies, and interchanged the names of their gods and goddesses. The underlying worship theme was toward nature, and most god-names were given to an aspect of nature.

In *Smith's Bible Dictionary* Smith says of nature-worship "... [it] recognizes male and female powers; whose symbols were the sun, moon and planets which has been said to have been the most complete and beautiful form of idolatry ever devised.... The worst feature of the system was the *sacrifice of children*... they [the nature-worshippers] believed in the development theory, that the first created beings were without intellect, and progressed from one stage to another up to man."[4]

Shocking press coverage today reports the breeding of children for satanic cult rituals, their murder in satanic activity, and the increase of missing children. Everything points to the rise of devil worship across the United States and Europe. The explosion of belief in progressive evolution and the rise in popularity of Wicca (witchcraft), and nature religions should warn us of macabre activity.

Venus Temple is dedicated to the Roman goddess of love, beauty, and fertility. Venus' Greek counterpart is Aphrodite.

Another Roman goddess Juno, is honored with Juno Temple. She was the patroness of women, marriage, childbirth, and family life (counterpart of the Greek Hera) and wife of Jupiter.

Jupiter, worshiped as a national god throughout Italy, was the principle god of the Romans, though not the creatorgod. He is acknowledged in the Grand Canyon with Jupiter Temple. He was identified with the Greek god Zeus and was considered to control the sky and weather, particularly lightning and rain.

Apollo Temple is set on an elevation of over 6000 feet. Although Greek in origin, Apollo was a major god of both Greeks and Romans. He is often depicted as the sun-god, and is patron of flocks and herds, archery, and arts (particularly music), and was seen as the god of prophecy, medicine, and divination.

Still praising the theme of nature, Thor Temple is strategically centered in Grand Canyon. Thor, the male counterpart of India's black goddess Kali, is one third of the old pagan European trinity. Wotan and Tiwaz are the other two aspects. (Interestingly, their names are preserved in our weekly calendar, Thor—Thursday, Wotan—Wednesday, and Tiwaz—Tuesday.)

Thor procured the most widespread devotion of all three and was represented as the savage, wild, chaotic god of thunder and lightning. He was the son of Mother Earth and was associated with agriculture. "In the late Northern paganism 'Black Thor' (from the color of his images?) was above all the enemy of the 'White Christ.' His sign, the hammer, was used in weddings and as a protective act, rather as Christians used the sign of the cross; and, as archaeology reveals, Christians took a cross to the grave, when traditional pagans took a hammer."[5]

Nature spirits and their controlling entities are referred to as "devas" by modern occultists. Freemason and modern occultist Madame Blavatsky's religion, Theosophy, regards devas with reverence too. (For more on Madame Blavatsky, see Appendix B.) Consequently it comes as no surprise to see Deva Temple perched in the Grand Canyon. According to Fred Gettings, "In the Zoroastrian cults the devas are actually regarded as demonic beings...but in the Indian cults they retain a wholesome and creative nature, being angels of considerable rank." Presumably following this homage, angels get there due in Bright Angel Canyon and Angels Gate.

The names of the gods of Ancient Egypt are included on the west side of the Grand Canyon. They exalt evolution and represent the worship of strong forces in the natural world. The Tower of Ra gives homage to the sun god Ra, who is said to be the father of Osiris, and is the very worship of Freemasonry in a mysterious secret ritual.

Osiris Temple pays respect to the god of vegetation, the cyclical force behind growth and decay. He was the brother and husband of Isis, the fertility and great mother-goddess.

Their evil brother Seth (deeply reverenced in many of today's satanic cults) is homaged in the Grand Canyon's Tower of Set. Set represents evil and the night, and in his furious jealousy of Osiris' power, he murdered his brother and stole his rulership.

However Isis conceived on her husband's dead body, brought him back to life, and bore a son, the sky god Horus. Horus defeated wicked Seth and resumed the lost rulership. The victor has a position of honor granted him in Grand Canyon's Horus Temple.

Eerdman's *Rapid Fact Finder* says of Osiris: "His wife searched for the pieces of his body and restored him to life. As a symbol of death and resurrection, Osiris became associated with life after death and the judgement of individual souls."

Pyramids, a significant symbol in Freemasonry, find their place in the canyon in Cheops Pyramid. Pyramids (Egyptian tombs) were the earthly encasement of a reverenced Egyptian god-man and his possessions enroute to the next world. Pyramids are a symbol of reincarnation, cousin to evolution.

In tracing the history of the naming of the formations in the "Big Canyon," as the Grand Canyon was known in 1870, and in attempting to discover the people behind the christenings, this writer stumbled on some interesting facts. At the west end of the canyon near Powell Plateau, at an elevation of 6200 feet, is Masonic Temple. In seeking to discover why the Freemasons had honored Powell with a commemoration plaque in 1913, the Masonic Grand Lodge of Arizona was contacted.

Interestingly, the commemorative marker placed at Powell Point by the Grand Lodge was donated to mark the fiftieth anniversary of the original Masonic initiation. Masons assembled at this holy site in the Grand Canyon to perform elaborate Masonic initiations and rituals on the Canyon's trails and peaks up until only 20 years ago.

The three important stages of Freemasonry were acted out on three varying heights of the National Park. This process symbolized the rising Degrees of Masonry. The ceremony included Initiation into the First Degree (Entered Apprentice), Passing into the Fellow Craft (the Second Degree) and the Raising into Master Mason (the Third Degree). The last is an obscene parody of Biblical water-baptism. Masonry is rooted in the idea of the Slain and Risen God, who they say was destroyed by an evil force and was resurrected by magic. The candidate of Master Mason is ritually slain in a mock ceremony on a rock in the Canyon and then raised as the Master Mason, god himself.

Many of the names of various pagan gods brandished around the Canyon are also used in Freemasonry secret rituals. The following quotes are taken from the doctrinal book of Freemasonry, *Morals and Dogma of the Ancient and Accepted Scottish Rite of Freemasonry*, by Albert Pike, Grand Commander, 1859-1891, and are intended to link names in the Grand Canyon with those revered in Free-masonry.

Osiris Temple. "Everything good in nature comes from Osiris —order, harmony, and the favorable temperature of the seasons and celestial periods" (page 4776).

Solomon's Temple represents one of the central themes of Freemasonry and is also the name of a rock in the Grand Canyon. Masonic ritual is concerned with the recovery of the "Lost Word," presumed to be the name of God. The Masons claim this word was lost through the murder of the architect during the building of Solomon's Temple. The Freemason's symbolic search for the lost word is an important part of the Royal Arch Degree.

No Royal Arch Mason can pronounce the whole sacred name by himself but three together can each pronounce a syllable. They pledge, "We three do meet and agree—in peace, love and unity—the Sacred Word to keep—and never to divulge the same—until we three, or three such as we—do meet and agree." It is then that the secret name of the deity of Masonry is revealed.

More Secrets Revealed

That secret name is Jaobulon. "Jao" is the Greek word for Jehovah. "Bul" is a rendering of the name, Baal (the supreme deity of Babylon). "On" is the term used in the Babylonian mysteries to call upon the deity Osiris.

Masonic loyalties to Egypt and the snake are quoted in *The Lost Keys of Freemasonry*[6] "Man is a god in the making, and as in the mystic myths of Egypt, on the potter's wheel he is being molded. When his light shines out to lift and preserve all things, he receives the triple crown of godhood and joins that throng of Master Masons who, in their robes Blue and Gold, are seeking to dispel the darkness of night with the triple light of the Masonic Lodge.

"The glorious privileges of a Master Mason are in keeping with his greater knowledge and wisdom.... For him the Heavens have opened and the Great Light has bathed him in its radiance. The Prodigal Son, so long a wanderer in the regions of darkness, has returned to his Father's house. The voice speaks from the Heavens, its power thrilling the Master until his own being seems filled with its divinity, saying, 'this is my beloved Son, in whom I am well pleased.' He [the Master Mason], in truth has become the spokesman of the Most High. He stands between the glowing fire light and the world. Through him passes Hydra, the great snake, and from its mouth there pours to man the light of God."[7]

On reincarnation, evolution, and communication with the dead (a practice condemned by the Bible) the book reveals: "It is not rational to suppose that the far nobler soul does not continue to exist beyond the grave: that many thousands who have died might claim to be joint owners with ourselves."[8]

Of Buddha, it says "The first Masonic legislator whose memory is preserved to us by history was Buddha, who, about a thousand years before the Christian era, reformed the religion of Manous."[9]

As previously mentioned, "It [Masonry] reverences all the great reformers: Confucius and Zoroaster, Jesus of Nazareth, and in the Arabian Iconoclast."[10]

The Canyon Honors Darwin

Darwin Plateau honors Freemason of high standing, Charles Darwin, the godfather of the theory of evolution.

Many unsuspecting Masons think that they can believe in biblical ideals and be Christians and Masons simultaneously. Their numbers have filled the pews of mainline protestant denominations for the last 200 years. Few Roman Catholics are Masons due to a pope's earlier mandate. In 1983, however, the Vatican lifted the ban on Freemasonry. And even some liberal Jews are now found to be involved in Masonry.

Although 75 percent of Masons do attend some kind of church because they have to believe in a supreme being, they are not "creed-bound."

"The true Mason is not creed-bound. He realizes with the divine illumination of his lodge that as a Mason his religion must be universal: Christ, Buddha or Mohammed, the name means little, for he recognizes only the light and not the bearer. He worships at every shrine, bows before every altar, whether in temple, mosque or cathedral, realizing with his truer understanding the oneness of all spiritual truth."[11]

Darwin, Freemasonry, and the Occult

Freemasonry tenets speak of "the Divine Nature and Wisdom, considered as the Deity of Success and Glory," from which flows "Dominion, or Rule," and which is "the reconciliation of Light and Darkness, Good and Evil." "The Will, as Wisdom or Intellectual Power... are really the Father and Mother of all that is; for the creation of anything, it was absolutely necessary that The Infinite should form for Himself and in Himself, an idea of what He willed to produce or create, to will was to create; and in the Idea, the Universe in potence, the universal succession of things was included. Thenceforward all was merely evolution and development."[1]

Upon comparing Freemasonry with the Bible, one quickly sees that the ideas of deifying nature, success, glory, and rulership are inconsistent with the commands of God. Worse yet, they are synonymous with the tactics of God's adversary, the devil. The idea that in God lie the "reconciliation" of male and female, of good and evil, and of light and dark is pagan and blasphemous.

Only in biblical perspective is God differentiated as all good and all light. In other world religions good and bad, light and dark are seen as two sides of one coin representing the character of God. Such conclusions are pagan, not Christian. Further Freemasonry concepts of "willing into creation and existence through intellectual power," are equally non-Christian. Creating one's own reality through mental maneuvering and imagination is nothing short of ancient witchcraft.

Darwin's quest for an alternative to creation would fit perfectly into the Freemason's agenda to destroy the biblical account of creation. Freemasonry does not believe in the God of the Bible that could create something out of nothing. Indeed Freemason's god is called "the architect of the Universe." And true to its definition, an architect must start with existing materials in order to build. Satan cannot originate anything but is only able to work with and twist that which is available to him.

Darwin's Occultic Connections

Interestingly enough, Darwin's affiliation with the occult did not stop with Freemasonry. Darwin's colleague and cofounder of the theory of evolution was Alfred Russel Wallace. Wallace, author of the book, *Miracles and Modern Spiritualism* was a devout occultist. While wandering in the tropics of the Amazon for 12 years, he became deeply involved in spirit rapping, table turning levitation, mesmerism, and automatic writing (he received letters from his dead brother in seances in his own home).

Wallace was an admirer of Madame Helena Blavatsky, organizer of the Theosophical Society in 1875. Blavatsky, along with such high ranking occultists as Annie Basant (suffragette and feminist) and Alice Bailey, were also Masons. There is within Freemasonry a branch which admits men and women as equals. "Droit Humane" (Human

Rights) was formed in the eighteenth century and championed equal rights for women. Droit Humane could be considered the predecessor of today's feminist movement. Modern co-Masonry is overtly occult, acknowledging the true Master of Masons as St. Germain, who was an Ascended Master and the Avator of the Aquarian Age.

According to German Orientalist Friedrich Max Muller, Theosophy expressed "the highest conception of God within the reach of the human mind, and the perception of the eternal oneness of human and divine nature."[2]

Blavatsky is considered one of the modern world's trailblazing psychologists of the visionary mind. According to social historian Theodore Roszak in his book *Where the Wasteland Ends*, Blavatsky influenced the Western mind toward a conception of moral, mental, and spiritual, as well as physical evolution. Her books reveal, he says, "the first philosophy of psychic and spiritual evolution to appear in the modern West."[3]

Blavatsky, occultist, spiritist, medium, and automatic writer, received messages from spiritual entities called "the brotherhood." In her book *Ancient Wisdom and the Universal Mystic Brotherhood* she wrote that the universe is composed of matter, spirit, and consciousness and is in a continual process of evolution. This idea brought together Theosophical thought with Platonic, Cabalistic, and Eastern sources—and ultimately modern Darwinism.[4]

Theodore Roszak notes that "Blavatsky's effort, unlike that of the Christian fundamentalists, was not to reject Darwin's work, but to insist that it had, by its focus on the purely physical, wholly omitted the mental, creative, and visionary life of the human race; in short, it omitted consciousness, whose development followed a very different evolutionary path."[5]

Wallace was an admirer of Theosophical evolution and enthusiastically picked up where Darwin left off. He saw the limitation of natural selection—that it could not explain aesthetic powers of the mind. Roszak notes that Wallace "agreed natural selection explains adaption; but in his eyes adaption was essentially conservative and unenterprising. It moves in a purely horizontal direction.... If evolution was merely a matter of survival by adaption, we might still be a planet of hearty bacteria.... Overlaying it Wallace saw a more daring vertical movement which boosts evolution toward higher levels of complexity and consciousness." Wallace asserted that this vertical movement was impulsed by a spiritual source.[6]

Wallace once wrote to Helena Blavatsky, commending her on her occult insight in *Isis Unveiled*: "I am amazed at the vast amount of erudition displayed...and the great interest of the topics on which they treat. Opens a whole world of new ideas and cannot fail to be of the greatest value."[7]

> Blavatsky, says Roszak, traces from the universal deific source to the incarnate human spirit. This immersion of spirit is for the purpose of vastly enriching our consciousness. "By our collective evolutionary course, and by innumerable personal incarnations, we make our way through all the realms of being: mineral, plant, animal, human, divine. And it is by virtue of this hard-won 'harvest of experience' that each human being becomes a microcosm of the universe...."
>
> It was Blavatsky's opinion that the perpetual

mysteries and missing links confronting scientists in every field will continue to plague them until the hidden side of nature, the occult cosmos is deemed a worthy subject of research. In *The Secret Doctrine,* she assures, however, that "there can be no possible conflict between the teachings of occult and so-called exact science where the conclusion of the latter are grounded on a substratum of unassailable fact. It is only when its more ardent exponents, overstepping the limits of observed phenomena in order to penetrate into the arcana of Being, attempt to wrench the formation of Kosmos and its living Forces from Spirit, and attribute all to blind matter, that the Occultists claim the right to dispute and call in question their theories.[8]

According to author Marion Meade in her book *Madame Blavatsky, The Woman Behind the Myth,* Madame Blavatsky claimed to have known Charles Darwin and translated his book into Russian while she was in Africa.[9]

Widespread attention propelled Darwin's reformation of an ancient religious concept into mainstream acceptability. The success is remarkable and has led many of Darwin's defenders to adulate him. Simultaneously, however, Darwin has been the recipient of much criticism from within his own camp.

Jacques Barzun, Columbia University's outstanding evolutionist historian, wrote: "Darwin was not a thinker and he did not originate the ideas that he used. He vacillated, added, retracted, and confused his own traces. As soon as he crossed the dividing line between the realm of events and realm of theory, he became 'metaphysical' in a bad sense. His power of drawing out the implication of his theories was at no time very remarkable, but when it came to the moral order it disappeared altogether, as that penetrating evolutionist, Nietzsche, observed with some disdain."[10]

NOTES

Chapter 1—Satan's Most Lethal Weapon

1. Richard Greene, J.D., Founder, Mind Expansion Institute, October 1, 1987 interview for the film *The Evolution Conspiracy: A Quantum Leap into the New Age*, (September 1988), Jeremiah Films, P.O. Box 1710, Hemet, California 92343, hereafter cited as *The Evolution Conspiracy*.
2. Paul Kurtz, ed., *Humanist Manifestos I and II* (Buffalo: Prometheus Books, 1973), p. xiii.
3. Willard Young, *The Fallacies of Creationism* (Calgary: Detselig Enterprises Limited, 1985), p. 82.
4. Ibid.
5. Richard Bozarth, "The Meaning of Evolution," *The American Atheist*, September 1978.

Chapter 2—Seducing the Masses

1. *False Gods of Our Time*, 1988, Jeremiah Films, P.O. Box 1710, Hemet, CA 92343.
2. Paul Blanchard, quoted in Marlin Maddoux, *America Betrayed* (Huntington House, 1984), p. 56.
3. Richard Hay and Mary D. Leakey, "The Fossil Footprints of Laetoli," *Scientific American*, February 1982, p. 50.
4. *Science* 162, October 11, 1968, p. 265.
5. Mary D. Leakey, "Footprints in the Ashes of Time," *National Geographic*, April 1979, p. 466.
6. Ibid., pp.448-49.

Chapter 3—Changing the Value of Human Life

1. From *Kinsey, Sex and Fraud* (Metairie, LA: Veras Books), as quoted in "The Sexual Revolution," *The Christian World Monitor*, June 1991, p. 11.
2. From *The McAlvany Intelligence Advisor*, as reported in "The Erosion of Morality," *The Christian World Monitor*, June 1991, p. 12.
3. Richard Ostling, "What Does God Really Think About Sex?" *Time*, June 24, 1991, p. 48.
4. Information on constitutional law was taken from a radio interview, "The Faith of Our Founding Fathers," with Dr. John Eidsmoe (Southwest Radio Church, P.O. Box 1144, Oklahoma City, OK 73101, transcript B-644). Dr. Eidsmoe has practiced constitutional law for ten years and is the Director of the Bill of Rights Legal Foundation, an organization whose goal is to oppose the American Civil Liberties Union.
5. Ibid.
6. Ibid.
7. Ibid.
8. Joseph Sobran, "The Averted Gaze: Liberalism and Fetal Pain," *Human Life Review* 9, Spring 1984.
9. Ibid.
10. Mary Senander, "Abortion As Birth Control: Pro-Lifers Shouldn't Make Exceptions," *Star Tribune*, February 27,1990.
11. Barbara Burke, "Infanticide," *Science 84*, May 1984, p. 29.
12. John White, *Christianity Today*, November 1990.
13. Henry Morris, *The Long War Against God* (Grand Rapids, MI: Baker Book House), p. 78.
14. Arthur Keith, *Evolution and Ethics*, in Morris, *Long War*, p. 147.

Chapter 4—Preparation for Delusion

1. Ian T. Taylor, *In the Minds of Men: Darwin and the New World Order* (Toronto: TFE Publishing, 1984), p. 34.
2. Walter Scott, *Life of Napoleon Buonaparte*, 9 vols. (Edinburgh: Ballantyne, 1827), vol. 1, p. 306.
3. Taylor, *Minds of Men*, p. 29.
4. Gavin de Beer, *Jean Jacques Rousseau and His World* (London: Thames and Hudson, 1972).
5. Taylor, *Minds of Men*, p. 54.
6. Michael Ruse, *The Darwinian Revolution* (Chicago: University of Chicago Press, 1979), p. 17.
7. D. Beales, *From Castlereagh to Gladstone 1815-1885* (London: Nelson, 1969), p. 68.
8. R.E. Schofield, "The Lunar Society of Burmingham," *Scientific American* 247, June 1982.
9. Taylor, *Minds of Men*, p. 55-57.
10. Ibid., p. 120.
11. Ibid., p. 67.
12. Helena Curtis, *Biology* (New York: Worth Publishers Inc., 1979), p. 3.
13. Taylor, *Minds of Men*, p. 66.
14. Loren C. Eiseley, "Charles Lyell," *Scientific American* 201, August 1959, p. 98.
15. Francis Hitchings, *The World Atlas of Mysteries* (Great Britain: W.S. Cowell Limited, 1978), p. 9.
16. Taylor, *Minds of Men*, p. 445.
17. Gertrude Himmelfarb, *Darwin and the Darwinian Revolution* (New York: W.W. Norton, 1968), p. 387.
18. Gavin de Beer, *Charles Darwin* (London: Thomas Nelson and Sons Limited, 1963), p. 45.
19. Ibid., p. 307.
20. Young, *The Fallacies of Creationism*, p. 105.
21. Michael Denton, *Evolution: A Theory in Crisis* (London: Burnett Books Limited, 1985), p. 25.
22. Charles Darwin, *The Autobiography of Charles Darwin, 1809-1882*, appendix and notes by Nora Barlow, granddaughter of Charles Darwin (New York: W.W. Norton and Co., 1958), p. 85.
23. David B. Wilson, ed., *Did the Devil Make Darwin Do It?* (Iowa: Iowa State University Press, 1983), p. 12.
24. Benjamin Jowett, *On the Interpretation of Scriptures, Essays and Reviews* (London: John W. Parker, 1869), p. 374.
25. Richard Freeman, *The Works of Charles Darwin* (London: Dawsons of Pall Mall, 1965), p. 21.
26. Taylor, *Minds of Men*, p. 354.
27. Ibid., p. 355.
28. Charles Darwin, *On the Origin of Species*, 2d ed. (London: John Murray, 1860), p. 481.
29. Hugh Miller, *The Testimony of the Rocks* (Boston: Gould and Lincoln, 1857), p. 179.
30. Thomas Chalmers, *Natural Theology* (Edinburgh: Thomas Constable, 1857), vol. 5, p. 146.
31. Taylor, *Minds of Men*, p. 368.
32. F. Darwin and A.C. Seward, *More Letters of Charles Darwin*, 2 vols. (London: John Murray, 1903), vol. 1, p. 191. Letter from Charles Darwin written to Charles Lyell, August 2, 1861.
33. Taylor, *Minds of Men*, p. 371.
34. Herbert Wendt, *Before the Deluge* (New York: Doubleday, 1968), p. 259.
35. Rev. Joseph A. Vadino, "Pope Discusses World Origins," *Saskatoon Star*, September 20, 1986. Column edited from the writings of Pope John Paul II.

Chapter 5—The Search for Proof

1. April Lawton, "The First Billion, Billion, Billion, Billionth of a Second," *Science Digest*, May 1981, p. 75
2. Paul Ehrlich and L.C. Birch, quoted in *Nature* 214, p. 352.
3. Peter Medawar, *Mathematical Challenges to the Neo-Darwinism Interpretation of Evolution* (Philadelphia: Wistar Institute Press, 1967), p. xi.
4. Henry Morris, "Evolution Is Religion, Not Science," *Impact* 107 (Institute for Creation Research, P.O. Box 2667, El Cajon, CA 92021).
5. N. Heribert-Nilsson, *Synthetische Artbildung*, 1953, quoted in Henry Morris, *Scientific Creationism* (San Diego: Creation Life Publishers, 1974), p. 9.
6. Colin Patterson in Morris, *Impact* 107.
7. Henry Morris, *Scientific Creationism* (San Diego: Creation Life Publishers, 1974), pp. 10-11.
8. Robert Jastrow, "Geo Conversation," *Geo*, February 1982, pp. 11-12.
9. Laurie R. Godfrey, ed., *Scientists Confront Creationism* (New York: W.W. Norton and Company, 1983), p. xi.
10. *Omni* February 1987, p. 44.
11. Isaac Asimov, "The Dangerous Myth of Creationism," *Penthouse*, January 1982, p. 120.
12. *Omni* February 1987, p. 49.
13. Frank Press. Letter written by Frank Press, President of NAS., received by Kent Intermediate School District, March 21, 1984.
14. Willard Young, *The Fallacies of Creationism* (Calgary: Detselig Enterprises Limited, 1985), p. 39.
15. Ibid., p. 36.
16. Phillip Kitcher, *Abusing Science: The Case Against Creationism* (Cambridge: MIT Press, 1984), p. 4.
17. Ibid., p. 176.
18. Ibid.
19. Isaac Asimov, "Atoms of Life," *Omni*, November 1983, p. 58.
20. Helena Curtis, *Biology* (New York: Worth Publishers Inc., 1979), p. 224.
21. *Webster's New World Dictionary*, s.v. "biogenesis."
22. Rick Gore, "The Awesome World Within a Cell," *National Geographic*, September, 1976, p. 395.
23. Luther Sunderland, interview for the film *The Evolution Conspiracy*.
24. Ibid.
25. Darwin, *Origin*, p. 168.
26. John Morris, "Did a Watchmaker Make the Watch?" *Acts and Facts* 10, March 3, 1990, (Institute for Creation Research, P.O. Box 2667, El Cajon, CA 92021).
27. Francis Crick, *Life Itself* (New York: Simon and Schuster, 1981), p. 88.
28. *The Incredible Machine* (Washington D.C.: National Geographic Society, 1986), p. 7.

Chapter 6—Missing Links

1. Frank Press, ed., *Science and Creationism: A View from the National Academy of Sciences* (Washington D.C.: National Academy Press, 1984), p. 23.
2. Louis S. Russel, interview for the film *The Evolution Conspiracy*.
3. Luther Sunderland, *Darwin's Enigma* (San Diego, CA: Master Book Publishers, 1987), p. 89.
4. "Whale with Legs," *Science Digest*, November 1980, p. 25. Illustration by Howard Friedman.
5. Wilson, *Did the Devil Make Darwin Do It?* p. 113.
6. *Science Year Book*, 1980, p. 292.
7. Ibid.
8. Sunderland, *Darwin's Enigma*, p. 77.

9. J. Millot, "The Coelacanth," *Scientific American* 193, December 1955, p. 34.
10. Francis Hitching, *The Neck of the Giraffe: Where Darwin Went Wrong* (New Haven: Ticknor and Fields, 1982), p. 34.
11. Press, *Science and Creationism*, p. 23.
12. William K. Gregory, *Science* 66, December 16, 1927, pp. 579-81.
13. Elliot G. Smith, "Hesperopithecus: The Ape-Man of the Western World," *Illustrated London News* 160, June 24, 1922, p. 944.
14. Taylor, *In the Minds of Men*, p. 233.
15. Donald C. Johanson, interview transcript for film *The Evolution Conspiracy*, June 1987.
16. Ibid.
17. Ibid.
18. Ibid.
19. Donald C. Johanson, "Ethiopia Yields First Family of Early Man," *National Geographic*, December 1976, p. 793.
20. Tom Willis, "Lucy Goes to College," *Bible and Science News Letter*, October 1987, p. 2.
21. Peter Gwynne and John Caley, "Bones and Prima Donnas," *Newsweek*, February 16, 1981, p. 76
22. *Time*, November 7, 1977, p. 41.

Chapter 7—God's Grand Design

1. Bozarth, "The Meaning of Evolution," p. 28.

Chapter 8—Children at Risk

1. Dr. Chester Pierce, at a Denver seminar on childhood education in 1973. Quoted in *Like Lambs to the Slaughter*, Johanna Michaelsen (Eugene, OR:Harvest House, 1989), p. 24.
2. Wilson, *Did the Devil Make Darwin Do It?*, p. 19.
3. Kurtz, *Humanist Manifestos I and II*, p. 7.
4. Ibid.
5. Ibid., p.8.
6. Ibid.
7. *Encylopaedia Britannica*, 15th ed., vol. 5., p. 680.
8. Marlin Maddoux, *America Betrayed* (Huntington House, 1984), p. 52.
9. Charles F. Potter, *Humanism: A New Religion* (New York: Simon and Shuster, 1930), p. 128.
10. Kurtz, *Humanist Manifestos I and II*, pp. 24-31.
11. Ibid., p. 13.
12. Ibid., p. 16.
13. Young, *The Fallacies of Creationism*, p. 20.
14. Wilson, *Did the Devil Make Darwin Do It?* p. 20.
15. Godfrey, *Scientists Confront Creationism*, p. 25.
16. Wilson, *Did the Devil Make Darwin Do It?*, p. 20.
17. Young, *The Fallacies of Creationism*, p. 39.
18. Ibid.
19. Ibid., p. 121
20. Wayne Moyer, "The Challenge of Creationism," *American Laboratory*, August 1980, p. 12.
21. Ibid.
22. Bozarth, "The Meaning of Evolution," p. 28.
23. Ibid, p. 30.
24. Kurtz, *Humanist Manifestos I and II*, p. 24.
25. Isaac Asimov, *Context Magazine*, June 15, 1982, p. 4.
26. Asimov, "The Dangerous Myth of Creationism."
27. "PBS Telecast Typifies Establishment Attack on Creation," *Acts and Facts* 11, September 1982, p. 1.

28. Moyer, "The Challenge of Creationism," p. 13.
29. Ibid., p. 14.

Chapter 9—Onward Evolutionary Soldiers
1. Jeremy Rifkin, *Algeny* (New York: Viking, 1983), p. 112.
2. Roger Lewin, "A Response to Creationism Evolves," *Science* 214, November 6, 1981, p. 635.
3. Press, *Science and Creationism*, p. 7.
4. Lewin, "A Response to Creationism Evolves," p. 635.
5. Ibid.
6. Ibid.
7. Kitcher, *Abusing Science*, p. 4.
8. Lewin, "A Response to Creationism Evolves," p. 636.
9. Ibid., p. 638.
10. "PBS Telecast Typifies Establishment Attack on Creation," *Acts and Facts* 11, September 1982, p. 5.
11. Wilson, *Did the Devil Make Darwin Do It?*, p. 198.
12. Douglas J. Futyma, *Science on Trial: The Case for Evolution* (New York: Pantheon Books, 1982).
13. Ibid., p. 5.
14. Ibid., p. 21.
15. Ibid.
16. Preston Cloud, interview transcript for the film *The Evolution Conspiracy*, June 1987.
17. Press, *Science and Creationism*.
18. Ibid., p. 5.
19. Ibid., p. 6.
20. Frank Press. Letter received by Kent Intermediate School District, March 21, 1984.
21. Lewin, "A Response to Creationism Evolves," p. 636.
22. *Omni*, February 1987.
23. Ibid., p. 12.
24. Quoted by Wendell Bird in interview for the film *The Evolution Conspiracy*.
25. "Ignorance 101," *Discover*, September 1988.
26. Vincent Sarich, interview transcript for film *The Evolution Conspiracy*, June 1987.
27. "A Religion for a New Age," *Humanist*, January/February 1983, p. 26.
28. Wendell Bird, interview for the film *The Evolution Conspiracy*.
29. Ibid.
30. California Department of Education, "The Science Framework for Californian Public Schools," 1990, front cover.
31. Ibid., p. xi.
32. "California Sued by Christian College, Creationism is Point of Dispute," *Los Angeles Times*, April 14, 1990.
33. "Science Teacher Files $5 Million Claim, Says Academic Freedom Thwarted," *Southern California Christian Times* (Mission Viejo), July 1991.
34. Ibid.

Chapter 10—A Quantum Leap into the New Age
1. Fritjof Capra, *The Turning Point* (Toronto: Bantam, 1982), pp. 77-78.
2. Shari Roan, "Great Expectations," *Los Angeles Times*, July 21, 1991.
3. John Randolph Price, *The Superbeings* (Fawcett Crest), p. 17.
4. Morris Cerullo, "Praise the Lord," broadcast on TBN, January 6, 1988.
5. Benny Hinn, "Praise-a-thon," broadcast on TBN, November 1990.
6. Kenneth Copeland, "The Force of Love" cassette tape.
7. Kenneth Copeland, "Following the Faith of Abraham" cassette tape.
8. Kenneth Copeland, "Believers Voice of Victory," broadcast on TBN, July 9, 1987.

216

9. Earl Paulk, *Satan Unmasked* (Atlanta, GA: Kingdom Dimension Publishers, 1985), p. 97.
10. Kenneth Copeland, "What Happened from the Cross to the Throne?" cassette tape.
11. Cavendish, Richard, ed., *Man, Myth and Magic* (New York: Marshall Cavendish, 1970), vol. 11, s.v. "Kali."
12. Michael McCarthy, "Dawning of 'Green Age' Shatters Old Certainties," *The Times* (London), December 29, 1989.
13. Gleaned from *Gaia* 1, (U.K.), 1990.
14. Jeremy Rifkin, *Algeny* (New York: Viking Press 1983), p. 244.
15. David Chilton, *Days of Vengeance* (Dominion Press, 1987), p. 58.
16. Gary North, *Liberating Planet Earth*, vol. 1 of *Biblical Blueprint Series* (Dominion Press, 1987), pp. 24,178.

Appendix A—The Grand Canyon's Mysteries

1. Phone conversation with a member of the Arizona Masonic Lodge, April, 1991, who said, however, that records were "poorly maintained at that time."
2. "Sages and Immortals: Chinese Religion," *Eerdman's Handbook to the World's Religions* (Grand Rapids, MI: Eerdman's, 1982), p. 246.
3. Ibid., "The Cosmic Battle: Zoroastrianism," p. 80.
4. *Smith's Bible Dictionary*, s.v. Phoenicia.
5. "The Old Gods: Religions of Northern Europe," *Eerdman's Handbook to the World's Religions*, p. 121.
6. Albert Pike, *Morals and Dogma of the Ancient and Accepted Scottish Rite of Freemasonry* (Washington, D.C., 1958), p. 4776.
7. Manly P. Hall, *The Lost Keys of Freemasonry* (Richmond, VA: Macoy Publishing and Masonic Supply Co., 1976), pp.92, 54-55.
8. Ibid., p. 539.
9. Ibid., p. 277.
10. Ibid., p. 525.
11. Hall, *The Lost Keys*, p. 65.

Appendix B—Darwin, Freemasonry, and the Occult

1. Pike, *Morals and Dogma*, p. 767. This esoteric book is to be returned upon withdrawal or death of recipient.
2. Cavendish, *Man, Myth and Magic*, vol. 20, p. 2814.
3. Theodore Roszak, *Where the Wasteland Ends* [Section: The Unfinished Animal] (Celestial Arts, 1989).
4. Howard Kerr and Charles Crow, *The Occult in America: New Historical Perspectives* (Urbana: University of Illinois Press, 1983), p. 119.
5. Sylia Cranston and Carey Williams, *Reincarnation: A New Horizon in Science, Religion, and Society* (New York: Julian Press, Crown Publishers, 1984), p. 34.
6. Ibid., p. 35.
7. Ibid.
8. Ibid., pp. 34-35.
9. Marion Meade, *Madam Blavatsky: The Woman Behind the Myth* (New York: G.P. Putman's Sons, 1980), p. 129.
10. Jacques Barzun, *Darwin, Marx, Wagner* (Garden City, NY: Doubleday, 1958), p. 84, from Morris, *Long War*, p. 152.

RECOMMENDED READING

Gish, Duane. *Evolution: The Challenge of the Fossil Record.* Master Books, 1985.

Ham, Kenneth. *The Lie: Evolution.* Master Books, 1987.

Hunt, Dave. *Whatever Happened to Heaven.* Harvest House Publishers, 1988.

Hunt, Dave and T.A. McMahon. *America: The Sorcerer's New Apprentice.* Harvest House Publishers, 1988.

Matrisciana, Caryl. *Gods of the New Age.* Harvest House Publishers, 1985.

Morris, Henry. *The Biblical Basis for Modern Science.* Baker Books, 1984.

Morris, Henry. *History of Modern Creationism.* Master Books, 1984.

Morris, Henry. *The Long War Against God.* Baker Books, 1989.

Morris, Henry. *Many Infallible Proofs.* Master Books, 1974.

Morris, Henry. *Scientific Creationism.*

Morris, Henry. *The Twilight of Evolution.* Baker Books, 1963.

Morris, Henry and Clark, Martin. *The Bible Has the Answer.* Master Books, 1987.

Morris, Henry and Whitcomb, John C. *The Genesis Flood: The Biblical Record and Its Scientific Implications.* Presbyterian and Reformed, 1961.

Morris, John. *Noah's Ark and the Lost World.* Master Books, 1988.

Oakland, Roger. *Evidence for Creation.* Whitaker House, 1989.

Taylor, Paul S. *The Great Dinosaur Mystery.* Master Books, 1987.

Whitcomb, John C. *The Early Earth.* Baker Books, 1972.

NATIONAL CREATIONIST ORGANIZATIONS

Bible Science Association
2911 E. 42nd St.
Minneapolis, MN 55406

Citizens Against Federal
Establishment of
Evolutionary Dogma
56 Beechwood
Plano, TX 75075

Creation-Life Publishers
P.O. Box 15908
San Diego, CA 92115

Creation Research Society
2717 Cranbrook Road
Ann Arbor, MI 48104

Creation Research Society
Books
5093 Williamsport Drive
Norcross, GA 30071

Creation Science Legal
Defense Fund
P.O. Box 78312
Shreveport, LA 71107

Creation Social Science and
Humanities Society
1429 N. Holyoke
Wichita, KS 67208

Films for Christ
R.R. 2—North Eden Road
Elmwood, IL 61529

Geoscience Research
Institute
Loma Linda University
Loma Linda, CA 92350

Institute for Creation
Research
P.O. Box 2667
El Cajon, CA 92021

FOREIGN CREATIONIST ORGANIZATIONS

Creation Science
  Foundation
P.O. Box 302, Sunnybank
Queensland, Australia 4109

Associacao Brasileira de
  Pesquisa da Criacao
Caixa Postal 37
Vicosa 36570
Minas Gerais, Brazil

Creation Science
  Association of Canada
P.O. Box 34006
Vancouver, British
  Columbia
Canada V61 4MI

Creation Science Movement
  (Formerly Evolution
  Protest Movement)
13 Argyle Avenue,
  Hounslow
Middlesex, England TW3
  2LE

Newton Scientific
  Association
3 Caernarvon Court
Caerphilly, Glam
England CF8 2UB

Somerset Creationist Group
Mead Farm, Downhead
West Camel, Yeovil
Somerset, England GA22
  7RQ

Bible and Science Press of
  Tokyo
4-41 I-Chome
Kaminito, Mito-shi
Ibaraki-Ken 310, Japan

Korea Association of
  Creation Research
15-5 Jung-Dong
Seoul 100, Korea

Ciencia y Creacion
Apartado 1759-A,
  Chihuahua
Chihuahua, Mexico

Creation-Science
  Association
Posbus 13816
Sinoville, South Africa 0129

Other Good
Harvest House Reading

GODS OF THE NEW AGE
by *Caryl Matrisciana*

There is a worldwide conspiracy threatening today's society. In a fascinating look at Hinduism and its well-disguised western counterpart, The New Age Movement, Caryl Matrisciana prepares us to be spiritually discerning in the days ahead. Must reading for every believer.

WHEN THE WORLD WILL BE AS ONE
The Coming New World Order in the New Age
by *Tal Brooke*

Today the pieces are falling into place for a worldwide transformation. In the not-too-distant future a New World Order, unlike anything the world has ever seen, could appear almost overnight. Could this be the global reality predicted 2,000 years ago by a prophet on the Isle of Patmos?

Tal is a graduate of the University of Virginia, and Princeton, and is a frequent speaker at Oxford and Cambridge universities.

AMERICA: THE SORCERER'S NEW APPRENTICE
by *Dave Hunt* and *T.A. McMahon*

Many respected experts predict that America is at the threshold of a glorious New Age. Other equally notable observers warn that Eastern mysticism, at the heart of the New Age movement, will eventually corrupt Western civilization. Dave Hunt and T.A. McMahon break down the most brilliant arguments of the most-respected New Age leaders and present overwhelming evidence for the superiority of the Christian faith.

Dear Reader:

We would appreciate hearing from you regarding this Harvest House nonfiction book. It will enable us to continue to give you the best in Christian publishing.

1. What most influenced you to purchase *The Evolution Conspiracy*?
   - ☐ Author
   - ☐ Subject matter
   - ☐ Backcover copy
   - ☐ Recommendations
   - ☐ Cover/Title
   - ☐ _____

2. Where did you purchase this book?
   - ☐ Christian bookstore
   - ☐ General bookstore
   - ☐ Department store
   - ☐ Grocery store
   - ☐ Other

3. Your overall rating of this book:
   - ☐ Excellent ☐ Very good ☐ Good ☐ Fair ☐ Poor

4. How likely would you be to purchase other books by this author?
   - ☐ Very likely
   - ☐ Somewhat likely
   - ☐ Not very likely
   - ☐ Not at all

5. What types of books most interest you?
   (check all that apply)
   - ☐ Women's Books
   - ☐ Marriage Books
   - ☐ Current Issues
   - ☐ Self Help/Psychology
   - ☐ Bible Studies
   - ☐ Fiction
   - ☐ Biographies
   - ☐ Children's Books
   - ☐ Youth Books
   - ☐ Other _____

6. Please check the box next to your age group.
   - ☐ Under 18
   - ☐ 18-24
   - ☐ 25-34
   - ☐ 35-44
   - ☐ 45-54
   - ☐ 55 and over

Mail to: Editorial Director
Harvest House Publishers
1075 Arrowsmith
Eugene, OR 97402

Name _____

Address _____

City _____ State _____ Zip _____

**Thank you for helping us to help you
in future publications!**